IMPRESSIVE COMMUNICATION
& SUCCESS MANIFESTO

SUBHASH KARTIK

I am grateful to all my mentors and
parents to whom I shall remain indebted
for setting the foundation on which
this book is based.

PREFACE

For a long time, I had been walking along the shoreline, but now the time has come to face the waves. I knew this new change would be hard and excruciating. However, I promised to have courage and learn new skills to face the waves and improve my life.
—Subhash Kartik.

WHAT KIND OF BOOK IS THIS?

This book practically represents how we feel and think about people, impressions, and income because we communicate what we think and feel outside ourselves.

Strange observation but true: I have never seen an arrogant, jealous, or sad person be an impressive communicator. Mind my words! Although they may be good at language skills, their characters, and their values, their arrogance hinders their growth. So, before you work outside and impress people, go inside first, correct yourself, and impress yourself.

HOW TO READ THIS BOOK?

This book will make you feel many inner value systems that you have but might not have examined so deeply. The tools and techniques being shared in this book will help you see what you lack.

A journey to improve your communication skills with **T.Q.P.S.** (the new communication system) will blow your mind, and the best part of the game is every chapter will bring micro change in you. Hence, you will have micro wins.

As you read, discuss the new system in each chapter with your spouse, partner or close friend. If not them, go to the most amazing person awaiting your attention: YOU. Do self-talk and discuss within until this new system is installed inside your mind. It is said that one who cannot talk to oneself cannot communicate with others.

START AN ACTION PLAN

One purpose of this book is to go within whenever possible and discuss your communication with yourself after every external communication. Ask yourself, " Did I speak well today with everyone?" "Could I be more articulate and speak with clarity during conversation?" You are the first person to evaluate your communication skills and give you the green signal.

Keep a notebook handy as you read this book, and mention what new things you learned from each chapter. What did you like the best? Becoming an effective communicator takes time; however, if you are ambitious and want to learn new skills and execute those skills.

You might often feel that the new communication system T.Q.P.S. is a bogus process, not up to the mark, and not fetching you fast positive responses, but you believe in this system; it has always worked and will work until the end. One should be committed to executing this new communication system. I have installed this new system and experienced remarkable changes in my personal, professional, and social growth.

When you finish reading this book, you will reach a Gargantuan Level of Communication. People will notice you, and you will cherish this new change in you.

CONTENT

PHASE 3 :   **THE CONCLUSION**

Personal Foreword by
Subhash Kartik for Excited Readers

Communication skills have been constantly in demand since people learnt to speak. The demand for this skill is so immense that most current leaders and aspirants eagerly want to improve their communication skills.

This book will **help Introverts** understand how to communicate effectively and leave their mark, even if they don't speak much.

Not only that, but **Extroverts can also learn effective communication hacks** to create a long-lasting rapport with others.

The communication game is less about quantity and more about quality. You can only present effectively in front of others when you have something effective and outstanding inside you. This book will provide you with all intrinsic, non-negotiable positive values and impressive tools, revamping your total personality and building a responsible and powerful communicator in you.

This book discusses the power of language, Neuroscience, Success, Communication strategies, Body language, and Core inner Values. It explains how these six important factors shape our lives and, especially, how we create our impressions in people's minds.

I had been waiting to write this book for a long time because I know how much I went through to improve my thought process, decision-making skills, and communication skills and become a coach through one of the finest skill training programs.

Subhash Kartik

If you want to be an effective communicator and impact people who knowingly or unknowingly follow you, then this book is for you. Believe me, it will give you a powerful personality, help you regain your self-respect, and help you attract your deserving goals.

This book is a perfect blend of Personal, professional and social communication and have no doubts saying this: this book will create awesome healthy relationships amongst your close ones.

As this is my first writing, I am extremely excited to pen my whole life experience into this book. The journey of becoming an effective communicator is not a hard but a tricky one. The despairing part of the Communication game is what others know and talk about; effective communication strategies are exactly the opposite of what communication exactly is, and I am so fortunate enough to put forward those tricky, not-so-popular, but impactful tips and techniques that will not only improve your communication skills but will transform your life game, people game and income game.

I have dedicated my life to making people amazing communicators.

Always approachable...
Subhash Kartik

P.S. To access all the live transformation workshops by me, you can also connect directly at coachingbysk@gmail.com

PHASE 1: REALIZATION

Time for Self-correction

Truth - 1
THIS IS NOT MY DADDY'S PLANET

When we communicate, we don't speak the message; one thing is even bigger than the message: Impression. Yes!

With every message we speak, we share our own impressions with people.

Imagine I ask someone whom you know, but not from your family but maybe your friend or one of your relatives or your colleague or boss or anyone less known to you and your behaviour, what will that person speak about you in your absence? What others will speak about you is what impression you have created in the minds of the people you meet daily, every week, every month. The next question or thought that might be hitting your mind right now could be. "That's none of my business what people think about me". No! Please never let this kind of statement enter your conscience; beware of that! Mind it, this is the only planet we share. So, we want or don't want, we can't stop thinking good about others. We shouldn't forget starting from our birth until we leave this planet, people have a BIG ROLE to play. Even our birth is the biggest plan made by two important people in our lives.

Can you think about your life without doctors, nurses, friends, employers, customers or service providers? People do matter in your life! Believe it or not.

Are you a blamer or a solution-giver? Think over it! Your blaming attitude can ruin your communication system. We are the results of our past decisions. When we cannot make decisions, we feel others are responsible for them. But the reality is simply the opposite. This is our life, and the final decision is always taken by us alone, whether reactive or proactive.

In my life, I wanted to become a singer; I learned Rabindra Sangeet for one year, and then my father told me to leave as this had no future, but I was fascinated by singing and won many certificates. But finally, I quit singing. I blamed my father for it. But today, I believe, "No, I decided to leave singing". Our parents can make some opinions about our lives and decisions, but the final go-ahead is always on our hands. I could have managed something if I wanted to become a singer that badly. I can't say right now how, but I could for sure. I could have begged, borrowed, or done something to fulfil my fascinating singing career. But the reality is, I did not badly want it.

Is there any story of yours related to blaming others for a long time now? If yes, please forgive him or her. Not only is forgiveness a great power, but it also gives you a wonderful personality that will always rise and shine. People around you will always be attracted to this kind of charisma.

Imagine having a cup of tea, and your kid is just running around. You warn him, but you know well that kids are the kings of their kingdoms. So, he ignores you, resulting in a minor mishap. Your cup falls on the floor and shatters into pieces. You get angry and shout at your kid with an insignificant question: "Who did this?" Imagine the situation when you know who did this. Then, why do you ask this question?

I mainly ask this question because I have a habit of blaming people. You might think your anger is normal in this case, but as I told you before, "what's inside goes outside." If you squeeze an orange, juice comes out.

Could there have been an ideal response to this statement—"Who did this?" I believe yes. We could also ask the kid, "How has it been done?" Wow! This sounds so mature and sensitive. Just read it two or three times; you will feel the difference.

When you deal with people, you deal with the most sensitive creatures in the world, and yes, you have to be sensitive, too, while talking. Imagine yourself: When someone talks to you rudely or you are blamed for your act, do you take it lightly or nicely? The answer is an absolute No!

This planet is for everyone. We all have the right to live according to our choices. But the "BIG BUT" is that when we deal with people next time, we must be more conscious. We will say what we want, but how we say it is the important rule of the communication game.

If someone does not care about people, he or she must make a separate planet for him or herself. So interesting, right? But it is serious! We don't have any right to hurt anyone by our words. People are not on the planet to entertain us, please us and take the burden of our own expectations. We all are here to live, love and lead.

Live with self-respect and respect for others, even the people we don't like. Love everyone who cares for you and be an example for others to live the same way. If anyone is a blamer or a misanthrope, they can never be an effective communicator. Misanthropes are villainous characters who never change their perspective about life and people.

I know some people are so nice until provoked, but the rule is the rule: Be respectful, assertive, and an example. Even be nice and talk nicely when you are hurt or heartbroken. Be the first person to say hi, talk, forgive, and transform.

So, we have to respect people; this is clear. But how do we talk to others? Don't worry. When your heart and mind start living, loving, and leading your way, your communication system will function naturally. You don't have to think about how to present yourself in front of them. You will see the magic of your own communication system, and people will like you, love you, and want you. You will be the Centre of Attention.

Our communication system is wonderful and like one of the universe's wonders. When you try hard to communicate with people just because you know it is important and must be done, your system will fail to obey you, and your listeners will never be impressed. Do what others will never do.

What do you think? What will others not do? Think!

When we go for an interview, most of us prepare hard. Isn't it? Now, my question is, what are you preparing for? You are preparing to present your best personality in front of your interviewer. Right?

It is fine to be ready and proactive. Imagine if you are always prepared to be nice, effective, communicate well, and be a proactive communicator.

Suppose you are not ready for life's unexpected events, and something negative happens. What will happen? You will fall apart, and your real communication system will sabotage your life. You will lose opportunities, people, and peace on this planet. On the other hand, you will see other people enjoying their roles on the same planet. So, be open to everything and be nice to people and the planet; the rest will be taken care of.

Don't try hard! If inside, you have compassion for people around you, your words and the presentation will be heart-touching. When you have nice feelings for others, others will feel your empathy.

Do not lose your charisma at any cost. Don't be restless playing this soft game with people; you will turn as hard as a rock. This game is not about convincing people, getting their approval, or being popular. This game is all about respecting others, empathizing with others, serving others being humble.

Dr. Seuss, an American author, once said these powerful lines...

Today, you are "YOU"; that is truer than true.
There is no one alive who is Youer than You.

Planet is for everyone; people are to be respected, listened to, and served, and you will see your whole life take an awesome turn and bring more success, prosperity and people ... believe me, really good people into your life.

Always remember, we attract everything into our lives through proactive, effective and impressive communication. Everything means everything. One beautiful day, your life will appear automatically happy, luckier and progressive.

Yes! We have superpowers to generate electromagnetic effects on the planet and create a positive or negative vibration in the hearts of people we meet and talk to. The choice is always ours and will always be ours. If we live a life with amazing rewards, we must communicate effectively with ourselves, the planet, and people.

They always say, "Save the planet".
I thought I always did. But today, I finally realize
the planet doesn't only mean "The planet",
but "The people" too. Thank God! Today I know
and it's not too late to begin.

– Subhash Kartik

Truth - 2
COMMUNICATION IS UNDERRATED

When did you first come across the fact that "Communication is important"? Chances are very high that, in those times, you were preparing for your higher studies or getting a job. Most people are unaware that "Communication is bigger than anything in the world". How?

Have you ever seen a person lose his job or not getting a job?

Have you ever seen a boy or a girl not getting marriage proposals?

Have you ever seen divorces taking place due to noise in the relationship?

Have you ever seen a salesperson who can't convince and get sales?

Have you ever seen a business person having no profits?

Have you ever seen everlasting family fights or sabotaging relationships?

Have you ever seen a lover who was not able to propose?

Have you ever seen someone who wants to say "No" but cannot do so?

Have you ever seen an employee unable to face his boss or superior?

Have you ever seen a kid's parents having difficulties talking to teachers?

Have you ever seen those parents who don't know how to talk to their kids?

You might be contemplating this right now. No doubt, these issues belong to the partial list. Many problems knock at our doors when we say, "WE GIVE DAMN TO PEOPLE AND EFFECTIVE COMMUNICATION."

Have you ever seen a highly qualified person who is incomeless? You have no doubt seen them. But If I ask you, "Have you ever seen an effective communicator without a job or income?" Think and think again... I have never seen such a person on earth.

You don't have to worry about anything when you have the finest communication skills. This is the only skill available on the planet, which is non-negotiable. The better you communicate, the more you impress people, the more you will be happy, and the more you progress in your life! Mind it! I am not talking about "speaking English" but effective communication. But yes, if you communicate in English effectively, you don't have to look back. Why didn't our parents tell us the importance of communication when we were kids?

Why didn't they force us to be effective communicators when we were in school? Why didn't they tell us, "Communication is a mandatory subject?" I wish they had told us more before. Maybe they joined the same bandwagon, and their parents didn't tell them the truth too. Anyways, Let bygones be bygones.

Now we know the secret, the importance, and that it's not about getting jobs but a wonderful life experience. 90% of our problems in life are based on our communication. So, gear up and start! This will take time, but results are guaranteed. We are already halfway through when we realize we must work on our communication; the rest will be easy.

I remember it was in class 8 when I went to a party with my parents. My parents spent time with their relatives, but I was looking for others my age, and eventually, I found them. I joined them but couldn't connect. I noticed they were speaking in English. I wanted to join in but couldn't. How could I? I was a student from a non-English medium school, and speaking English was not my strong suit.

English communication created more personal problems in my life. I used to ask my father, "Why didn't you put me in an English-medium school?" and my father had no answer.

It is said that "if you haven't invested in yourself, especially in your communication skills, it will be difficult for you to be an effective communicator." Why is this investment important? Most of us learn communication from our parents, friends, teachers, and relatives, which we never choose so critically. So, the chances are very high that my communication can be as good as those I meet regularly. But the reality is, "my company is not my territory".

I need to learn from a communicator, not just anyone I meet, to be an effective communicator. If I need an expert's help in communication, I have to invest. Investing in our knowledge and skills is difficult because most people don't know the importance of self-investment. Even the decision to buy this book is an investment you made. Now, you have to evaluate the return on your investments.

When did I come to know the importance of communication? Although I faced many issues while communicating, I was never so serious about my own communication until I met my friend Pratichi (now my wife). She was my neighbour and used to study in an English medium school. Many such conditions occurred when we met: she started speaking in English, I replied with the wrong English grammar, and I was stopped multiple times. It is really very difficult to get negative feedback from your friend about your communication, especially when that person is your special friend… hmmm … will talk about her later. So, by now, you have learned that I faced most of my language and communication issues in my personal life only.

Many confident English speakers often fail to impress others. This shows language is just a medium to speak. Language is an entry gate but not an impressive gate. Being competent in English always gives us an edge over other speakers, but making people love ourselves needs a magic game, not a language game. Do you want to learn this magic game? If yes, then choosing this book could be one of the best decisions in your life.

People who struggle with communication and fail to impress people often face personal, professional, and social issues in life. The problem is not that they cannot impress others but that they are not willing to work on their communication skills. No willing results, no learning. This proves why the chapter is titled "Communication is always underrated!"

Do you like salespeople? Do not say "No"! I believe a salesperson inside us always tries to sell himself to others. Sometimes, he sells his points to his elders, he sells to get a job, he sells to his close ones to get trust, and most of the time, he fails. Do you know why? He fails because he sells only. He never cares for people. Believe me, I hate to sell. I do feel when you care for people, you don't have to sell. You serve and create an impact.

Are you in pain right now? Are you facing any challenges in your life, or do you have any pain areas? Following and executing TQPS communication systems in your lifestyle will surely help you overcome all your challenges.

Many times, when my friends and relatives share their life tragedies, and I tell them to organize their communication skills, they never take me seriously. I used to feel bad being unheard earlier, but communication is my focus today. However, that doesn't mean I can make others feel the same.

Anyway, if everyone starts working on communication skills, then everyone will be successful in life. Thank God communication is still very much underrated. Not everyone is serious about communication, but you are!

Anyone who has taken communication so seriously and put enormous effort into improving their communication skills can never be a simple human being. A mission to communicate effectively and respect people is not something popular nowadays. This is the mission of a real hero, and I salute them!

Communication needs to be mastered!
He who masters communication,
comes out of all delusions,
and join the heroic mission.

— Subhash Kartik

Truth - 3
JUST GO BEYOND

Many people approach me and ask me to make them an extrovert like a magician. Ha-ha-ha-ha… Some ask for valuable tools and techniques to become an extrovert person. But here is a big question – Is this important to change our personality traits? If I am an Introvert, do I need to become an extrovert? Or extrovert to introvert? As per my experience, the right answer is "BIG NO!"

Since childhood, I have been an introvert. Whenever I talked to someone, I felt a lack of words. I was shy. However, my elder brother was very different from me. He was very extroverted, used to talk more, and could easily gel with people. Even our relatives liked him more than me because he was so smart. I don't know why I didn't dare to face people. Later, I realized that I am an introvert and very shy. But I was wrong!

My thought of being introverted was right, but claiming myself to be shy was my biggest mistake. There is always a difference between an introverted person and a shy person, which I came to know later. I studied human characteristics and found many unknown truths about Introverts and extroverts, which made me feel good about myself later.

I was wrong! I used to feel that being an extrovert was the best personality trait. But no one told me that being an introvert or an extrovert doesn't matter. Both traits are God-gifted and hereditary; we must accept, approve, and recognize them. My whole school and college life went into feeling that I was a shy person—the most ineligible person.

Finally, I came to realize who extroverts are. Extroverts love to speak. They are very expressive. They think less but speak more. Comparatively, Introverts love to listen but talk less. Rather, it has been seen that introverts talk to themselves (self-talk) more and more. Yes, this is right! Introverts talk to themselves more, question more, and sometimes guide more.

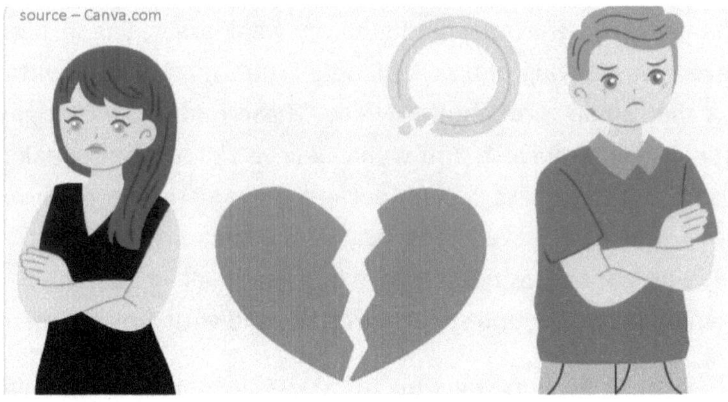

Extroverts are more vocal; sometimes, they say something that is not supposed to be said. In some cases, they experience major relationship issues. They even lose people in their lives. On the other hand, introverts always think beyond themselves. Introverts think multiple times before speaking in front of others. So, the question arises again: Who is the best—an introvert or an extrovert?

Let me share some of the rarest cases when you see extroverts having some noticeable traits of introverts, like speaking less, looking sensible, and listening to people more with more attentiveness. Even the same magical changes you see in introverts, too, like they speak more and are found with more sociable traits. In this case, many people fail to find the exact personality in them. But how is this possible? It becomes possible when extroverts and introverts decide to be "better than their natural personality". This change is a transformation that is not found every time in everyone. In this situation, extroverts and introverts change their negative traits into positive ones. They work hard on their weak points. When these personality types negotiate with themselves and decide to work against their weak areas, they revamp themselves to be ambivert personalities.

Being an introvert, I started working on my weak areas, like facing people almost every day, saying hi first to people I met, making eye contact, and keeping a mild smile throughout my day. These minuscule changes made my personality an ambivert. You won't believe I didn't just speak more. I kept myself as before, less spoken but more expressive through my body language. I knew very well that language impacts only 7%, but body language, eye contact, smiles, and expressions all impact 55%. So, go beyond language, go beyond speaking, go beyond your limiting personality.

Even when an extrovert personality starts listening to people more attentively, speaking only about the important things, letting others speak and letting others complete their sentences, by applying these courses of action, extroverts transform into ambiverts.

No doubt extroverts and introverts are blessed to have amazing attributes, but they always must work on their weak areas. Being an ambivert provides an option to go beyond. Ambiversion is the best application to be performed personally, professionally, and socially.

There is a big question for you: who are these shy people?

You might think people who do not speak or interact are shy. This statement is not completely right. Shy people are those who are passive in their body language. Yes, body language. You heard it right! Passive body language, what does it mean? Some people who never smile, keep their hands on their pockets or back, feel reluctant to make eye contact with others, and always walk backwards… are shy. Shy has nothing to do with talking or interacting. On the contrary, if these shy people start smiling, walking forward, making eye contact and using their hands, they will be taken as more interactive and social people.

Few say that introverted people are shy, which is not true. It has been seen that introverts who smile and make eye contact, even though they speak less, are never told they are shy. Can you believe this? Being shy means showing no communication at all. But when people start using impressive body language like smiling, making eye contact, using their hands, and walking forward, they are welcomed by society. Maybe that is why we say, "Body language is more important than just a language." Do not just take these words; follow and execute them to see the drastic changes in your personality.

Being an introvert, I took a step beyond my natural style. I started my own Edupreneurship initiative in the name of IDQ Value Adder Academy in 2008. I started rendering life-changing training programs on Communication Skill Development, Personality Dev. and Corporate Excellence Program.

In my Educational entrepreneurship journey, I have interacted with more than 10 lakh students, almost 1 lakh corporate employees, and entrepreneurs. Believe me, I never spoke beyond what was needed, but I communicated every time with my body language and voice modulation. Yes, even "YOUR VOICE" matters... it is said to impact 38%. You can't ignore this fact.

I have seen many speakers whose language skills are amazing but fail when communicating and impressing people. Most of them focus on language and information. Yes, that is important, but apart from information, there is one more thing in BIG DEMAND: "Impression," which comes from how we deal with people with our impressive body language and conviction-based voice.

If anyone reading this book feels he or she is an introverted person, please take it as a blessing because introverted people are sensitive, better listeners, better self-talkers, creative and even focused. Accepting your own identity is the first step towards success.

If you are an extrovert, you have to feel good because the almighty has bestowed many positive qualities on you, and the best one is that you know well how to befriend someone more easily. You feel it is your finest skill among all skills. But yes, next time you open your mouth to speak anything, ensure you think about the listener or audience and then proceed. If we don't think twice before we speak, we may upset someone with our words.

Dealing with people is extremely sensitive. But yes, becoming and applying ambiversion should be the best choice for everyone. So, go beyond introversion and extroversion. Be an Ambivert! Start working on your communication style. Push yourself to the result you want. This may not happen automatically, but little forcibly. There is nothing wrong with doing the right thing forcibly.

Next time, whenever you can face people, FACE THEM, WALK TOWARDS THEM, SMILE TO THEM... BE THE FIRST PERSON TO SAY HI! Yes, these little changes will create a massive positive response from others. You do not need to speak more, but genuinely look at them and show some respect and love towards others. Rather, people who speak more are never taken so seriously.

Here, I am not talking about extroverts. All extroverts are not Obnoxious. Now, what is the word "Obnoxious"? Obnoxious people talk in unpleasant ways, unpleasant things. They need help. Obnoxious people are always criticized.

So, finally, we should always remember that introverts are not shy, and extroverts are not obnoxious.

The best version of the personality is always going beyond… "Be an Ambivert!"

Speak less, Listen more

Speak less, Smile more

Speak less, Eye more

Speak less, Hands more

Effective Communication demands
I less, you more!

- Subhash Kartik

Truth - 4
THE HALF COMMUNICATOR

Is this possible for a person who is a very effective communicator in the office but, at the same time, a rude communicator at home? Or the opposite condition? The answer is Yes; many such examples are found in real life. Most of us know effective communication is an important tool to impress others. We know we have to be polite; we have to be respectable, we have to be understanding, but when it comes to our practical life, even if we want to be polite, respectable, or understanding.

However, we fail to do this. How is it possible that the same person is different at home and opposite in the office? Does that mean some communicators are playing double roles?

Are they 50% effective and 50% ineffective in communication?

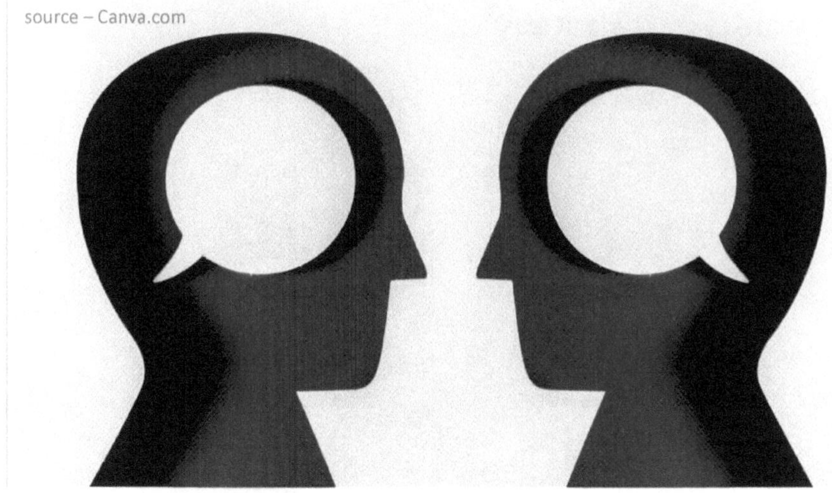

The name of this chapter is "The Half Communicator, "which means half effective and half ineffective. But again, the same question: Is this phenomenon possible in real life? It might be, but real people with value systems will always be patient, positive, polite, and passionate towards their esteemed listeners, whether at home or in the office. Listeners are always important, and taking care of them, giving them the respect they deserve, and speaking with care is the utmost responsibility of a speaker. Not every speaker believes this. Some try but fail.

Why not everyone is patient, positive and polite towards the next person? Does that come from a superiority complex? From where does this superior feeling come? Experts have found when our pride and arrogance take over us, we think "we are the gods". We think, "Others are at my service". We think, "We are controlling others' lives". Never let this attitude hit our brains. If you have such feelings, constructively do self-talk, for example, "I have achieved, and now I have everything I want, but I should not forget the contribution of my family, friends, and clients towards my goal and achievements. Without them, I could never have reached where I am now. I owe them my gratitude at least".

Half-Communicators are doing good in their lives, not extraordinary. Either they are good and nice to their family, or they are nice to their organization. Both ways they lack balance in their lives. Self–realization is important first to overcome this superiority, but self-realization is not a popular word for others. Self-realization comes from TQPS. The full form of T.Q.P.S is the Total Quality People System.

TQPS is a tool for managing your values. First, TQPS needs to be installed and then the same needs to be balanced. During installation, we need to know which values are universal and which should not be messed with. In future chapters, we will encounter outstanding values that govern our lives. After installation, value management needs to be executed, and every value needs to be read and practised daily.

Values always affect the communication process. For example;

Positive people speak positively and constructively.

Caring people speak with care and compassion.

Jealous people talk skeptical and blame people.

Angry people talk angrily and aggressively.

If someone is cool in the office but irritable at home, something is wrong. If someone talks amazingly in the office but rudely at home, something is wrong again. If someone teams up with colleagues in the office but doesn't care about anybody in the family, there is a massive problem in the Half-communicator's life.

This book has been written to galvanize all Half-Communicators into Impressive Communicators. The journey will be challenging, but Phase 2 – Rebuilding strategies are more powerful than commonly available tips and techniques on the same topics. If you know any Half-Communicator, gift him this book, and that person will be thankful to you for your entire life.

PHASE 2: REBUILDING
Time for Skill Installation

Truth - 5
VOCA – BULLY

How much would you rate your vocabulary? Vocabulary plays a big role in communication. You can talk about any language, be it our mother tongue, Hindi, or the most demanding language, English. If your vocab is not improved or regularly revamped, you will face difficulties impressing your audience with your language skills. It has been observed that most students work on their vocabulary until age 25. After that, we become busy with our professional struggles and personal responsibilities.

Studies show that language is 7% efficient, but using unique and awesome-sauce vocabulary will get your attention. You might have been amazed when the word awesomesauce was used.

The best practice is learning at least one new vocabulary word daily. But where would you find it? The best and most sophisticated places could be your daily newspaper, magazine, TV show, Google, or YouTube. There are plenty of sources, and the time required is also minuscule. However, we need to realize the power of that new word, which could gargantuanly impact our communication.

The chapter name is "Voca-bully"; the reason behind giving this name was to make sure you improve your vocabulary and be vocal or get bullied. What if we are learning English, speaking fluently but using the same boring words daily? Using new words will get you social proximity. Nowadays, proximity is power, and our communication plays a pivotal role in creating our social stature and network.

To take your vocabulary to the next level, you have to use **V3-Technique**. Visualizing, Verbalizing and Vitalizing. Visualizing is the first step, where you get a new word, see the word, and see the letters more attentively. See the lines or curves in that particular word and relate the word to a picture. For example, suppose the new word is "eavesdrop". This word means "listening to someone's talk secretly". The visualizing process starts with visualizing a picture of someone eavesdropping on someone. If I get a picture, it's good, or I can imagine the same thing. Visualizing will help us to picture the same word inside our brains. Especially when we imagine a word with a picture, our right brain gets triggered and helps our brain to store the new word inside our subconscious brain, and when our conversation demands that word, it will come naturally to our mouth while speaking.

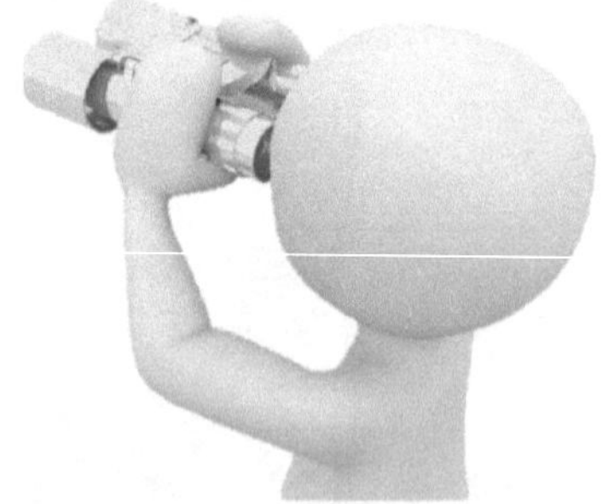

Next comes Verbalizing, the second step in which we speak the same words multiple times, sometimes only in a sentence. Sometimes, we spell the word forward, and sometimes, we spell backwards. This process helps us store the word "eavesdrop" inside our brain and helps our tongue get used to speaking this new word whenever demand comes.

And finally comes the last step, Vitalizing. In this step, you speak and use this work in different types of sentences, for example.

I am eavesdropping on their conversation.

Do you like eavesdropping on people?

Don't you eavesdrop while sitting beside them?

I shall never try to eavesdrop on anyone.

He will never be eavesdropping during our meeting.

Using the words in different types of sentences, even different tenses would also help us to be competent and confident during our conversations. While talking about the V3 technique in this book, we have done all three processes; as a result, you know the word "eavesdrop" and will never forget the same. You must follow this easy technique and impress people with your immaculate vocabulary.

Be vocal with a fresh, new, impressive vocabulary.

Or be ready to be bullied by the adversary. The choice is yours!

Truth - 6

B.E.S.O.F.T. OR BE DEAD

Body- language is always over-spoken but under-delivered. We all know Body language is crucial for communicating clearly and effectively. The best part is that body language is natural. We don't learn it, but do it. Even newly born babies easily communicate with body language and convey their message to their parents. We can mask our words with sophisticated lies (lies with logic and excuses), but can we mask our body language? The answer is BIG NO!

How to be a powerful but at the same time likable communicator using our body language? There is a method called - **B.E.S.O.F.T.** You won't believe it; this method is so damn powerful and Result-oriented that even when an introverted person applies This method makes him or her look like an extrovert communicator without speaking much (at least not a shy speaker). So, what is B.E.S.O.F.T. method?

B.E.S.O.F.T

B – BE AT AN ANGLE

While speaking with others, it's very important to show some respect and importance to the listener—our posture matters. The way we sit and talk can make a big difference. Imagine I am talking to my client and sitting with an upright posture. Think for a moment about how that would seem. Sitting upright and talking to anyone shows superior posture as if I am trying to outshine the person. Even sitting at a backward angle is also not recommended because that shows inferior posture. So, the best posture is to sit and keep your body posture at an angle so your body can lean towards the listener.

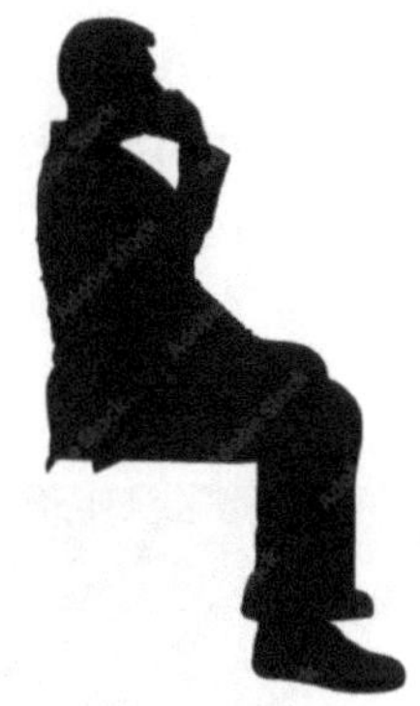

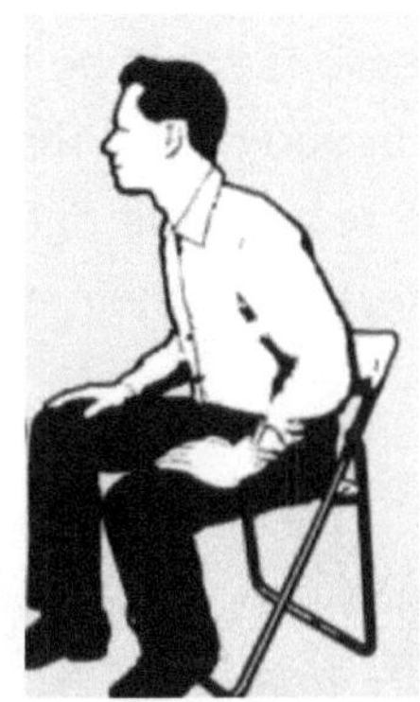

Sitting Upright and talking   Leaning forward and talking

Even when sitting beside anyone, you can lean a little forward sidewise to show interest towards the person beside you. These little proactive postures do big magic. Your positively inclined postures show respect for the other person, showing Interest and self-readiness. This is a positive body language one can showcase during communication (equally effective for standing posture, too).

E – EYE CONTACT

Eye contact with the person with whom we are interacting is non-negotiable. If you speak with conviction and confidence but fail to make eye contact, others will have a repulsive effect. During one-to-one or group discussions, keeping eye contact with the person speaking and listening is crucial.

What if you are uncomfortable making eye contact while talking to someone?

Sometimes, you might not feel comfortable making eye contact with others. The reasons could be that you don't like that person, you want to ignore them, or you do like that person but feel shy about talking to them. Whatever the reason, the right solution is to face people even if you are uncomfortable, look at their eyes, and speak.

S – SMILE

Smiles uplift our face value. Without a smile, we look like robots; there is no life on our faces without a smile. Smiles bring relief to people suffering from acute tension and stress. Have you ever observed how people respond to our smiles, knowingly or unknowingly? Try this out: When you smile, others respond positively—at least most do.

Now, the question is, do you smile for a reason, or don't you need any reason to smile? Before you think about your answers, I want to clarify something important. If you smile for a reason, the reason might not last long, but if you do not have any reason to smile, you are free to smile every time without thinking about reasons.

Why do people smile when they are happy? Why don't you smile every day? Here, every time means whenever I want to. Even if you talk about reasons, I personally feel we have numerous reasons to be happy. Don't you believe this?

For instance, right now, I am writing this book. I am super happy because publishing a book was my long-awaited dream. I am happy because I am healthy mentally and physically. I am so fortunate to eat three or four times a day. Wow! I am in my bed right now, which is so comfortable. I have an amazing house to stay in. I can see my family around me, and they are happy.

The more I try to search, the more reasons I find to be happy. Happiness is blessed upon all of us; few who seek it get it, and those who doubt it miss out.

O– OPEN GESTURE

What if you speak but never use both hands? Are you sure you use both your hands impressively while speaking to someone? Do you know that using both hands while speaking or presenting creates a confident and bold picture of yourself? At the same time, using both hands will help the audience understand the content more accurately and effectively. Using both hands while speaking keeps your audience alive during your talk.

If someone is uncomfortable using their hands, they can keep both hands near the chest area, creating a triangle-shaped position, keeping both hands a little open and moving as per the words used by the speaker.

If hands are locked near the chest area, we are not open to speaking to anyone or do not like speaking to a particular person. Often, hands become a burden to speakers, but in a real sense, hands work as an effective weapon for the communicator.

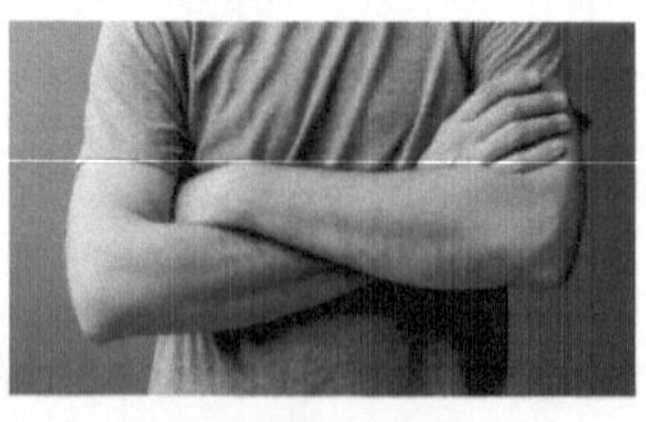

Hands are locked

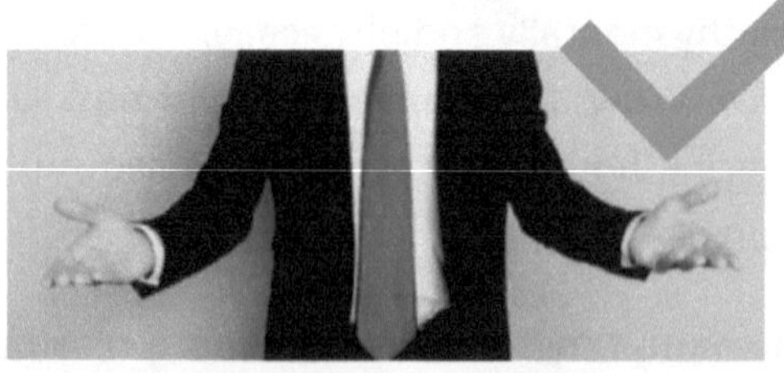

Open gestures (both hands openly)

F – FORWARD NODDING

If someone could make an extra effort to nod his or her head back and forth to clarify understanding while listening to someone attentively and empathically, no doubt everyone would be impressed. Attentiveness shows that the listener is not distracted and monomaniacally focused on the speaker, and Empathy shows that the listener feels the speaker's inner feelings with the same intensity.

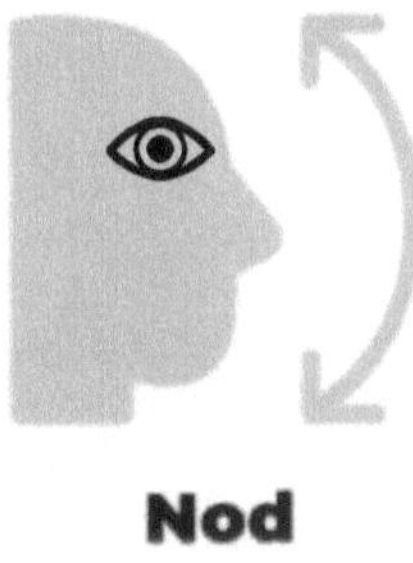

Nod

Everyone loves to be heard; everyone loves to be given importance, and everyone loves to be pampered. So, give them (speaker) what they want by simply nodding back and forth when listening. Ensure the Listener should perform Nodding with proper eye contact and a mild smile on their face.

T – TOUCH WITH CONVICTION

When was the last time you shook hands with anyone with conviction and the other person was impressed? Do you feel confident when you shake hands with others? Do you feel confident when you shake hands with strangers? Do you feel confident when you shake hands with your senior colleagues or boss? Do you feel confident shaking hands with someone of your opposite sex? If your answer is "Yes", that would be great. Keep it up! Or if your answer is "No", there is a caution! Your feeble handshake might have been considered the result of your feeble personality. Your weak handshake can ruin your impression, income and self-respect.

While making a confident handshake, your fingers should grip the other person's palm, and your handshake should be firm. Ensure your handshake is not bone-crushing or feeble at any cost. The right way to shake hands is to lean slightly forward, smile genuinely, offer your hand to the other person, and bend your elbow slightly. Ensure your thumb points to the ceiling, both palms close, and finally, touch the other hand firmly with all your fingers.

Even if time and situation demand, we might have to fake our confidence until we have our confidence. If your mind is uncomfortable shaking hands with someone, use your body! Use your hand! Use your knowledge! Use your skill of shaking hands. Fake it till you make it.

Truth - 7
SQUEEZE THE ORANGE

What comes out when we squeeze an orange?
Guess the answer!

What are you thinking?
Let me clear the air, yes! you are right "It's juice."

When we squeeze an orange, juice comes out.
Now, a little deep question: what comes out when life squeezes you?
Yes, I am asking you – dear reader, what comes out?

It is very simple: if you have lies, dishonesty and manipulation,
Those come out simple.

If you have fear, hesitation, hate or revenge, those come out?
Those come out if you have apathy, a negative attitude or arrogance.
Isn't that simple?

Now, if you have all the above negative
Characteristics: can you impress people?

You know the answer. Right?

Let's deep dive inside you; yes, my reader, "your inside".

What's there? Love or hate? Loyalty or treachery? Revenge or hate? Integrity or manipulation? Respect for self or disrespect? Arrogance or humility? Proving mentality or improving mentality? Self-love or self-blame?

Your answer can't be "both"! Your answer could be "mostly."

But whatever your answer could be, your "Impression" will always be (in the minds of others) on the negative side.

People who hate can't impress people!

Treacherous people can't impress people.

People who manipulate can't impress others.

People who disrespect themselves and others can't impress people.

Arrogant people can't impress people.

People who always try to prove can't impress people.

People with a self-blame attitude can't impress people.

So, what should be your next step?

Simple, don't speak the way your mood is.

Don't speak the way your habit pokes you to say.

Don't speak the way your money and designation instigate you to speak.

Don't speak the way your obnoxious nature might trigger you to say.

Don't speak the way your bad times impel you to say.

Speak less Impress More

Speak "What is Right"!
Speak the way Total Quality People speak!
Speak the way Dignified People speak!
Speak the way Generous People speak!
Speak the way Empathetic people speak!

Speak with a Quality System: There should be a system that is not politically, socially or economically driven but "Self-Driven".

We call it – T.Q.P.S.

T.Q.P.S. – TOTAL QUALITY PEOPLE SYSTEM

Mostly, people speak the way their circumstances impel them to say. Many people are either servants of their life situations or some rare ones are Quality Driven, Value Driven and Self Driven. T.Q.P.S. creates masters. T.Q.P.S. creates leaders, and T.Q.P.S. transforms energy vampires into leaders.

T.Q.P.S. can only be engraved in our minds with the help of – **Gargantuan Personality Advantage (G.P.A.)**

If **G.P.A.** can be installed inside our Value system, it will cause a **Gargantuan Shift** in our personality, communication skills, and mindset.

Our Gargantuan Personality will help us impress people and get noticed, even in a crowded, competitive, and crabby world.

Our Gargantuan Communication Skills will help us to get into the hearts of people who are important to us.

A gargantuan mindset will help us attract wealth, happiness, and growth in life.

So, are you ready to experience this **GARGANTUAN SHIFT?**

I know your answer—it is "Certainly"! Right? Then let's proceed, but before we start, one precaution: The GPA journey will be hard, initially messy, and confusing. Later, you might feel "bogus," too.

But the outcome will be – Yes!
… you guess it right!

The Gargantuan shift in your life.

Gargantuan Personality Advantage (G.P.A.)

5 Value System: We need to install GPA into our system ASAP!

Value System 1 - INTEGRITY

Value System 2 – DIGNITY

Value System 3 – POSITIVITY

Value System 4 – EMPATHY

Value System 5 -?????? …. can't say right now; this is life-saving

Let's start with the basic … the foundation

<u>**Value System 1 - INTEGRITY**</u>

What is Integrity?

Simple and basic answer – Think about what is right. Do what is right and speak what is right. No condition applies.

Some people are smart—sorry, not smart, but fiendish. They do and speak about what is right just to get noticed. In their thought process, they think, "I will do right and speak right when people will notice me. If no one notices me when I am doing right or speaking right, what's the use of following Integrity?"

I guess Integrity can be confusing; let's change the definition a little –

Think about what is right, do what is right, and speak about what is right even if no one is watching. Yes! Now, this is clearer!

What do you say? Are you thinking, doing, or speaking right most of the time, if not every time?

Now you might wonder, what is "Right"?

For one person, "something" could be right, but that "something" might not be right for the other. Are you getting this?

Let me take you through my life when I was 16…

I was studying, and the next day, I had my exam. I was never very studious, but I used to be a little more during exam time. So, I was studying just one day before my exam. My father came and said, "Lovy*, you have to go to the market to bring some important stuff."

*Lovy is my nickname (it sounds like- Love + e = Lovy)

The story continues: My father wanted me to go to the market. I was obedient, listening to almost everything my parents said. My nature was also **to** be a good son, brother, and friend, so I never said "No" to anyone. I used to feel that saying "No" was bad, and selfish people used this word.

So, when my father told me to go to the market, I said, "Yes!" It was simple. I am a good boy. What did you expect me to say? Why should I say "No!" to my father? He can never go wrong.

But the question is, did I want to say "Yes"?
Did I want to go to the market?
Did I want to obey my father at that time?

The actual and right answer is – "NO!"

Oh no! Did I use the word "No!" here? Have I done right?

 Have I become a bad boy now?

Ha, ha, ha... I am laughing right now as I write this book. I was thinking about how stupid I was. My childhood was spent pleasing people and saying "yes" to everyone. I never respected myself, stood up for my rights, or stood up for the best person in my life—

Let's go to flashback...

I wanted to become a singer, so I also took training. I won many awards, too. But finally, my father said, "No! These are time and money wasters," and I said, "OK, Papa, you are right."

I wanted to become a cricketer. I used to bowl fast. I thought of learning, and I even started learning cricket, but finally, my father said, "No! Focus on studies." I said, "OK, Papa, you are right."

I wanted to become an actor, so I started taking theatre training. I also started working as a main actor in a small regional music album, but finally, my father said, "No! Focus on studies. Good people don't go into the film and movies." I said, "OK, Papa, you are right."

So, in my life, I could have become a singer, a cricketer, or an actor, but all my dreams went to waste just because I could not say that one word, "No" to my father. Can you believe it? What can happen if you can't say "No?"

Oh, I forgot to continue my father's and my conversation...

I was studying for the next exam when my father said, "Lovy, you have to go to the market to buy some important stuff." I wanted to say, "No!" but I could not, so I finally said, "Yes!"

I didn't realize that by saying "Yes" to my father, I indirectly said "No!" to myself. Isn't it?

Finally, I said, "Yes!" and left my studies to go to the market. While going to the market, I talked to myself negatively and talked negatively about my father. My mood was negative, my learning mindset was negative, my exam preparation was negative, and my exam was negative. My relationship with my father grew negative, and finally, my self-respect went for a toss.

Just because "I couldn't say "NO!" to my father. Can you believe this?

I used to curse at my father for this during those times, but today, I realize it was my mistake, not my father's. I couldn't say "NO!" to him. I should have had the Integrity to respond to my father rightly. I chose a good path, not the right one. Today, after learning about integrity, I won't repeat what I used to do in the past.

My relationship with my family, especially with my father, is much better than before. This has to be. If we do right, nothing wrong can happen to us. We might have to have patience, sometimes more patience, but the results will always be positive and right. Integrity never fails.

The old question arises: How do I know what is right? How do I know what I am doing is right? What if I am doing wrong but think I am doing right? Oh my god. Now, this Integrity is getting more perplexing.

Never forget this – How do I know what I am doing right is right?

Ask yourself three questions to check whether you are right or not.

First, When I do something right, I love it. I enjoy the process, and it makes me feel amazing and delighted. I do not give it a second thought and can do it for long hours. Right now, I am writing this book. I love this, and I can do it for hours.

Second, while doing what I love or happily do, can I help others and receive blessings? Am I able to offer a value proposition to others? Are people benefiting from my work? The benefits could be physical—they are getting something out of me—or mental—they are getting something like peace, happiness, and relief. I am writing this book right now, and I know many will gain power and heroic benefits from it.

Third, Whatever I am doing is progressive. Is it helping me grow constructively? This growth could be in learning, wealth, designation, relationships, or health. Likewise, if my book can impact the lives of others, they will buy it, and I can generate revenues from it.

So, Integrity was and has always been easy to understand, but, yes, it is not so easy to execute in our lives. But once you embrace Integrity inside you, your positive reaping will start. This might not reduce your problems, but it will give you a solution and make you better, stronger, wealthier and more peaceful.

So, **do what is right!**

Finally, following Integrity doesn't mean "I have to say No to everyone". Absolutely not!

This is more like – when saying No is right, say No! When saying Yes is right, say yes! Follow what is right, not who is right.

Keep practising Integrity; believe me, you might fail even after practising what is right, but keep practising.

When everything fails, Integrity wins. When people fail, Integrity wins. When life fails, Integrity wins.

So, Integrity is non-negotiable.

Value System 2 – DIGNITY

Do you follow the **11/90/90 RULE**? Have you ever heard about it? Ok, I will talk about this later.

Dignity is self-respect. Do you respect yourself? You might feel "Yes".

Very good!

Let me measure your Dignity. I will ask three simple questions, so don't worry!

You have to answer with "Yes" or "No".

Out of those 3 Yes or No answers, If any one of those answers comes out as "No", it will signify you failed Dignity.

Are you ready? Be double sure! Are you ready? Let me ask then.

Before you get to know your dignity level, it's important, whatever the result comes, if you fail or pass, to accept it first, give your approval to change in case you fail, and transform it with the required tools to organize your dignity. Tools will be provided, so chill.

Here are those three life-changing questions –

Question 1 – Are you among the happiest people on earth?

Answer hint: This doesn't mean you don't have problems in life, but you manage all your problems and stay happy. So, what's your answer? Are you happy?

Answer now: Yes or No?

Question 2 – Are you among the luckiest people on earth?

Answer hint: This doesn't mean whatever you want, you get that easily and immediately. This means you believe in your life. You believe there is a superpower that listens to your wishes. Who has given you when you least expected? Sometimes you get it immediately, sometimes you get it lately, and sometimes you do not even get it, but you always believe in that superpower. So, what's your answer to this? Are you the luckiest one?

Answer now: Yes or No?

Question 3 – Do you feel you are progressive?

Answer hint: Have you progressed in the last five years? Do you get any daily signals that you are growing in your career, job, or business? Have you been feeling that your personality has become more organized? You look better now. You sound better now, and people feel better with you. Your bank balance has grown, too. Do you feel this?

Answer now: Yes or No?

If you have answered all with "yes", awesome – salute to your dignity.

But cheers to those having difficulties saying yes or failing dignity, too! At least you know you have to transform. At least you know this is possible. At least you know there are remedies. So, you have dignity, or you don't have one, follow below 11/90/90 FORMULA to ensure dignity for your entire life and make your life dignified.

11/ 90 / 90 FORMULA

11 – 11 Rules to create a dignified life for self

90– 90-minute daily execution of 11 Rules without fail (non-negotiable)

90– Follow these 11 Rules every 90 minutes for the next 90 days

UNLOCK - 11/ 90 / 90 FORMULA:

<table>
<tr><td>11 RULES</td><td>RULE : 1

FORGIVE SELF & OTHERS</td><td>RULE : 2

SAY NO! WHEN IT IS RIGHT</td><td>RULE : 3

FOLLOW RETICULAR ACTIVATING SYSTEM (RAS)</td></tr>
<tr><td>RULE : 4

BE MONO-MANAICALLY FOCUSED AT WORK</td><td>RULE : 5

RECKON – LAW OF SUPPLY</td><td>RULE : 6

HEAL P.R.</td><td>RULE : 7

VALUE DRESSING</td></tr>
<tr><td>RULE : 8

JUSTIFIED QUALIFICATION</td><td>RULE : 9

20 MINS. MOVE , MEDITATE & MANIFEST</td><td>RULE : 10

MINDFUL VALUE SLEEP</td><td>RULE : 11

MINDFUL VALUE EATING</td></tr>
</table>

When you start following this 11/90/90 formula, chances are high that you will get bored, sometimes feel messy, and be about to quit. That will be where you need to stay hard and clinch the process.

So, are you ready to execute 11/90/90?

Before you proceed, tell yourself, "I am ready. It is hard but worth it, and I will do it."

RULE 1: FORGIVE SELF & OTHERS

Why do we doubt ourselves? Why do some people always lose? Why do some people quit even before attempting something? Why do some people stay sad and demotivated? What are their stories and tragedies? Don't they want success, progress, happiness, money, and prosperity? The answer is they do. Then what stops them?

Most of the time, their inner child is scared, upset, angry, or broken. But why? Maybe the reason is their own bad or wrong decisions in the past. They are still holding on to their past. They have not forgiven themselves yet.

source – Canva.com

What next is very simple to do but hard to start. First, sit silently, ensuring no distractions and no people around. Take your right hand on your chest, a little towards the left side, below your left shoulder and close your eyes. Breathe deeply for 2 minutes, feel your breath and tell yourself -

"I made many mistakes. I admit this and have taken a lot today, but now I am ready to shift to a Gargantuan life. I am ready to shift to a happy and lucky life. I am ready to shift to a progressive life, so I am ready to forgive myself for my past decisions, my past negative thoughts, and even old toxic relationships".

"I am ready to forgive all those people who made a hell out of my life."

"I am ready to forgive myself, and as I can forgive myself, I can forgive everyone who hurt me and my life in the past."

Do this every morning, before you start work, when you walk, when you breathe, and even before sleep. Continue doing it for 90 days and work on 11 other rules. You will feel something is getting healed inside. The beauty of this process is that you will feel many instant changes when you do it. There will be changes in your neuroscience, such as your body's chemicals, hormones, and neurotransmitters. This is the prime rule of the game before you go to the next rule; this rule#1 needs to be executed well.

I, your author, truly want your forgiveness through you.

RULE 2: SAY NO! WHEN IT IS RIGHT

After learning Integrity, one thing is set: I will think about what is right, do what is right, and speak what is right. Considering this Value System, from now on, we have to learn to say "No!" if it is right. If I want to say "No" to another person but finally say "yes" to him or her, this means indirectly I am saying "No" to myself.

Are you getting this? Read the line again to understand the cruel reality of life. It is fine if saying "yes" to others does not affect me or my life. But if saying "yes" to others affects my life negatively, I will wake up and correct myself. Stand for my rights! No one will do it for me. I have to stand for my Self-respect. Saying "no" when it is right is one of the greatest powers; rare can do it, but whoever does it feels high about themselves.

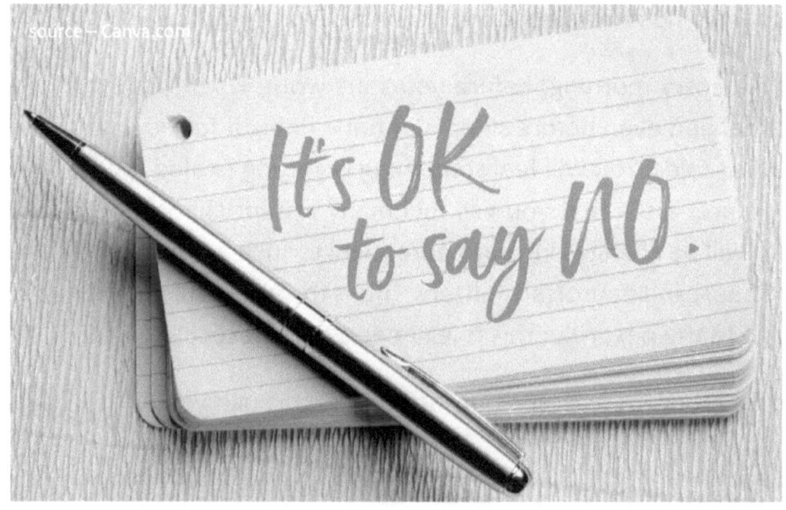

Ensure that when you say "no" to others, you say it politely, with a mild smile and positive body language. Saying "no" does not mean "I am not with you"; rather, it means "your statement is not aligned to my integrity" is very simple.

There is a difference between disagreement and disrespect. Disagreement is absolutely fine. We are different people with different thought processes. We may disagree with someone else's thoughts, but disrespect is against Integrity. I may not like someone or feel angry seeing someone, but integrity means talking right, behaving right and responding (reply) right.

When we say " no, " we don't have to be bad, rude, or dominating. Rather, we need to be more caring, loving, and alert to the extent that our "no" should not affect someone else's self-respect.

Start executing this rule#2 every day. Sometimes, we might have to say "no" to ourselves when we are not doing right. Yes! for instance, every morning, we need to go out and exercise, so we must wake up and go. But this doesn't happen every day. We might have to fight with our fiendish mentality, which stops us from exercising, meditating, self-reading, etc. In that particular time, we need to stand against ourselves and say "no" to our weak self, who loves our comfort zone, who love to be lazy and sleep whenever possible. So, sometimes our enemy lies inside us only, especially for those inner lazy instigating enemies; stand and speak with integrity and say that one word, "No!" and start doing "what is right".

RULE 3: FOLLOW R.A.S.

If someone asks you a common question, "How are you?" what do you answer?

I am good, fine, or as usual, or fine …

Through these above answers, you attract mediocrity in your life. Because what you say makes your day.

When you say, "I am good" or "fine," you want to tell the person, "My condition is as usual, like others, nothing special."

Through these answers, you are attracting average life and average people. Why average life? Because your answer is very common, nothing unique, when you answer with these common words, indirectly, you tell people, "I am not special; I am just like others".

These low-standard average (LSA) answers often hinder connecting with high-standard, unique (HSU) people. HSU people are found less in the crowd and are undoubtedly noticed and popular. When HSU people meet LSA people, they get low vibration, so they talk and connect less. There is an amazing line in English: "Proximity is power". Our connections often create magic in our lives. But our connections are not always so magical and progressive. So, to connect with those HSU people with high positive vibrations, we need to create HSU vibrations.

Now the question is, how do these HSU people create high positive vibrations? From where and when do they get so much positive vibration? The answer is that HSU people create positive vibrations through their continuous focus and repetitive positive self-talk with themselves.

For example, if HSU employees lack money, they never say, "I don't have money."

They say, "I am working on money; money is on the way. I am working on it".

If HSU people fail, they never say, "I failed." They say, "What should I do next? Let's try this or that. What next?"

If HSU people fail in a relationship, they never say, "People don't love me. They leave me". They say, "What have I done? Do I need to correct myself? I might have to try again. I am ready to admit my mistake. I should forgive her".

If HSU people don't get what they want, they never say, "I am unlucky". They say, "If I have not gotten what I wanted, I have to try again. Maybe I don't deserve it right now, so I have to upskill myself and make myself more deserving. I know I will get it, if not immediately, but for sure. Let me be focused".

Finally,

If HSU people get the question, "How are you?" they never say, "I am fine". They say, "I am superb, mind-blowing, top of the world" (not only do their words have magic, but even their energy is effervescent, too).

The secret of their HIGH-STANDARD EFFERVESCENT PERSONALITY is their focus. HSU people always focus on "What they want", not "What they have or are". Read again this particular paragraph.

HSU people always say, "Wherever our focus goes, energy, results, and progress flow." Sometimes, to create this HSU vibration, HSU aspirants fake it until they make it. Although faking is not what we promote, faking for a good reason, for positive energy, or for what we want to feel has always given surprising and desired results.

Now, the question is, what is RAS? RAS is a Reticular Activating System. A Virtual Intelligent System (VIS) inside our brain. It helps us see what we want, hear what we want to hear, and finally, feel what we want to feel.

So, when we want to feel good, even in a negative environment, VIS makes us see, hear, and feel positive vibrations.

For instance, you might know or have seen me, or we might have talked in the past. Now imagine the time before you even knew me or knew my name. In those times when neither my name nor I was inside your brain, could it be possible that we both crossed paths but couldn't recognise each other? Can this be possible by any means?

The answer is, "It is quite possible; we can't deny it." This means that it might also be possible that if we don't know what happiness, luck, or progress is in real terms, even if these things cross paths in our lives, we cannot recognise them. If we don't create happiness inside our brains, we can't enjoy it; the same goes for luck and progress.

So, believe in RAS and pursue your best, desired, and deserving life. When you achieve the best life, you start respecting it.

RULE 4: BE MONO-MANIACALLY FOCUSED AT WORK

Do you believe in "Mono-maniacal focus"?

This means focusing on one thing at a time and giving your full energy and time to work on that.

Do you believe in multitasking? What would you choose if you were given a chance to become a multi-tasker or an expert tasker?

Multi-taskers, who do many works at a single time, are fast, and they save time. But the question is, when your attention is divided into multiple tasks, can you give your best out of all tasks?

Conversely, when you do one thing at a time, and you give your time, energy, focus, knowledge, skills, and even your love and affection, you create a Virtuoso inside you. Virtuoso is a term given to those who are experts and irreplaceable.

There are exemplary performers like Amir Khan, Shahrukh Khan, Amitabh Bachchan, Madhuri Dixit, Lata Mangeshkar, A.R. Rehman, Arijit Singh, Sachin Tendulkar, Ratan Tata and many more. These great names are famous and liked not for their multi-tasking but for their mono-maniacal focus on one thing, whether acting, singing or writing, making music, serving society, etc. No one can even think of replacing them for what they have done.

Monomaniacal-focused people are always in demand. They are knowledge and skills experts and people seek their help, even paying them big.

When you focus on one thing, even that thing, what you focus on, seeks you back, respects you, and gives you back with the desired results. Always remember, "What you seek, it seeks us back". When multiple people come to you to seek your knowledge or skills or help, your self-confidence and self-respect will go super high. You will realize your importance in the organization and society where you work and live. Do read this paragraph again.

RULE 5: RECKON LAW OF SUPPLY

There are two types of people: one who believes in abundance and the other who believes in scarcity.

The law of Supply talks about abundance. As per the Law of supply, there is plenty for everyone.

When I started my organization IDQ in 2008, I worked, earning, and growing alone. Later, my partner joined in 2018. We all started working together, so no doubt revenue was also getting divided.

The situation became more complex when my third partner joined me in 2019; revenue got divided again. Although the organization was small, our revenue and per-head income were still limited, although we had three partners. I started feeling low and disappointed. Sometimes, I felt even after 10 years of my organization, I was nowhere. I was seeing scarcity everywhere. However, I started reading more and getting more guidance from my mentor. Finally, I realized my downfall was not the result of adding partners but adding more scarcity in my thoughts, negative feelings, and negative focus, and I decided to change and correct myself.

When time is hard, it's very difficult to correct self. It's rather easy to blame others and sleep. Anyway, I am a dead follower of my mentor, Robin Sharma; he said something big would come across my path if I focused on supply and abundance. So, finally, I decided to see abundance everywhere, even in nothing.

Started focusing on Supply rather than scarcity. Started using statements like "Good things are on the way; I can feel it" rather than "Nothing good happens in my life". Believe me, the Law of supply works. Believing in supply and abundance works; believing in oneself, even when results seem blurry or negative, really works.

So, always believe that what you want is what you get, even if it's not what you want. Focus on what you want, give your full attention to it, and finally, your 100% efforts (karma) should add to what you want.

RULE 6: HEAL P.R.

When we focus on our work more than our personal lives, we often overlook who is surrounding us and adding to our lives tremendously. They could be our family or friends, sometimes relatives or somebody who is not your blood relation but heart relation.

I remember, in 2020, when I started feeling growth in my business and got a feeling of success for the first time, suddenly my health started deteriorating due to lack of sleep and bad eating. I suffered anxiety attacks and depression. I was losing my health, energy, and interest area, and sometimes I felt – I was going to lose my life (feeling of death). Then I realized how important my health is and how important my family is. During those difficult times, only my family were by my side. I still remember my parents being awake at night and helping me feel good. I remember my wife took all my responsibilities and managed the kids single-handedly. Even my elder brother used to come to my house and give me all kinds of head and leg massages to make me sleep (because I had not got sleep for almost 6 months, even though it sounded a little unbelievable). Sometimes, we are so busy during our good times that we overlook our close ones.

Take a moment to consider your life. If something bad happens, who will be by your side? Your boss, customers, colleagues, friends, or family? You know your answer.

Feeling family around us brings us joy, courage, and high energy. A thousand trophies and millions of dollars in a bank account would make no difference if we feel "alone." We might sometimes feel that money can replace people, but we are humans, the most emotional creatures in this universe. We can be happy with money for a few days or months, but eventually, we will run for a relationship, especially when we are short of money, health, or nostalgia.

So, it's important to have PR (Personal Relationship) protected from our professional achievements and positions and glories. If your personal people are on your hate list, it is already too late to forgive them, so do it fast and Heal Your Personal Relationship. If you are on their hate list, then first forgive yourself and ask for forgiveness from your own people. They will surely forgive you one day, if not now. That's family; little initiative is always important. Be the first person to forgive and heal your relationship.

RULE 7: VALUE DRESSING

Dressing is important from two perspectives: self and others e.g., anyone who meets us, sees us, or talks to us face to face. First, they see us and make an impression. Dressing could be a little conscious or unconscious, too. Conscious dressing means you are alert, you know where you are heading to, why you are going (the purpose), and even when you are going (occasion or day or time). Unconscious dressing means dressing is not on your priority list. For you, dressing means covering the body, not more than that.

Our dressing sense creates an impression, and an impression creates income; I always say this. However, not everyone succeeds in creating a long-lasting positive impression. Following the TQPS (Total Quality People System) makes you special, like a brand.

A brand goes through multiple breakdowns and creates a breakthrough out of it. A brand runs through tenacity, creativity and value proposition (how can I serve others with what they want).

When you are a brand and wear anything worn by anyone whose values are not aligned with TQPS, your values are questioned and doubted, not theirs. But just in case, imagine you are a brand and are associated with a brand that follows TQPS, too. Imagine the Powerful, Confident, and Likable brand you will become and the transformation and impact you create.

Next time, don't just wear a dress; go Value-Dressing. Beware! Before you choose the Right Dress, choose the Right Values through TQPS.

RULE 8: JUSTIFIED QUALIFICATION

Are you working? Or are you a businessman? Are you qualified? What is Qualification? What does Qualification talk about a particular holder of that qualification? Is there any difference between qualification and education?

Are you a housewife? What qualifications do you have as a housewife? Is your qualification helping you? Do your kids know your qualifications? Do your neighbours know your qualifications and degrees you have?

Answering all the above questions might be minuscule to you, but the main eye-opener is that if I am qualified, I have a degree or a certificate in a particular subject. That's not a paper only about that particular holder holding that degree with designated knowledge and skills.

A degree signifies that the holder justifies that degree and has all the important knowledge available and expected out of that degree.

If somebody has a Degree on B.Sc. Zoology means that a person has almost all possible knowledge and insights. Justified Qualification means that if I have the degree, I should be able to perform what that degree demands. But if we always consider passing the exam, just getting a minimum number, what big can I serve with that certificate, even if I pass? Then what is education?

Education is the real knowledge and wisdom. Many don't have degrees or certificates but know. For example, Rabindranath Tagore was the first Indian and Asian to win the Noble Prize in Literature in 1913, but what was his qualification? History says he had dropped out of school because he didn't like the four-walled classrooms.

Many successful people did not go through scheduled schooling arrangements and became renowned speakers, motivators, or businessmen. How did they do that? It's very simple: "They gained knowledge in their line of interest and simply loved their interest area." They might not have the right certificate but have the right knowledge and wisdom.

So, are you justifying your qualifications? Do you have all the necessary knowledge and skills to perform your job in the domain you are working in (business or service)?

In short, are you justifying the monthly salary you are getting for the accountabilities you have been assigned to do in your organization?

Think again and again. Just working for money is mediocrity, or it leads us to mediocrity. When you work to serve people and give value propositions to your customers or the organization, you justify your qualifications.

RULE 9: 20 MINS. MOVE, MEDITATE & MANIFEST

Intense exercise, meditation, deep breathing, and self-study on self-development books for 30 minutes are not negotiable. Self-respect demands Self-management. If we don't manage ourselves, saying "I respect myself" is just hype, not a true hope for a Heroic life.

Intense exercise, brisk walking, yoga, aerobics, etc., elevate our metabolism, cleanse toxic hormones inside our body, and help raise our neurotransmitter dopamine and endorphin levels. But still today, many people say, "I am doing exercise to burn my fat", where burning fat is just a secondary reason. Then why should anyone do exercise? Primary reasons are still unknown to many or may be ignored by many.

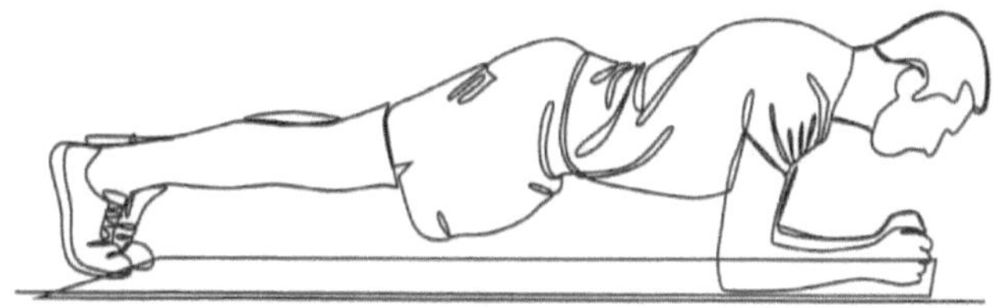

Many people still don't know that the more we exercise, the more focused and energetic we will be, the more our brains will be optimized, the more productive we will be, and the longer we will live.

Meditation and deep breathing help raise the oxygen flow in our body, especially in our brain. This heals our body and brain both. Our happiness lifts, and wisdom is developed optimally. We experience peace and high creativity. It decreases our reactive thinking and elevates our proactive thinking. We feel more ready for upcoming challenges. Due to high creativity, our performance touches a gargantuan level, and we experience a richer life. I (your author) wish I had known all these 20 years back, but I started in my 30s and never turned back.

Can we manifest anything we want? Does Manifestation work as Aladdin's Jinn, if manifestation works, how long does it take to execute our wishes? There are many questions and confusion, but one thing that still holds the show together is that Manifestation is real, and we can manifest anything. But how?

Manifestation takes place in 3 phases, 1st Asking, 2nd Believing and 3rd Receiving:

Asking:

Ask what you want. Ask the universe. For instance, my current body weight on 1 January 2025 is 120 kg, and I am asking the universe, "I want to have 60 kg by 31 March 2025." My ask is undoubtedly specific, but is that realistic? Is 60 kg burning in just 90 days realistic? You decide that.

Our ask should follow SRT (Specific, Realistic and Time-bounding). You can "ASK FOR" anything related to your personal life, professional life, or social life that can be manifested; the only thing to be ensured is SRT.

Believing:

The whole world is asking from the universe; how does the universe select your "asking" over others? Does that mean the universe also selects demands among many? The answer is "Yes! Why not".

The universe sees 3 things –

(a) To what extent (karma & Creativity wise) can you go to get what you want?

(b) How desperate you are to get what you want (in the sense of facing failures and disappointments) and finally

(c) How much can you trust the process of "Believing" in the self and Manifestation itself (even after your karma and failures get you nothing)?

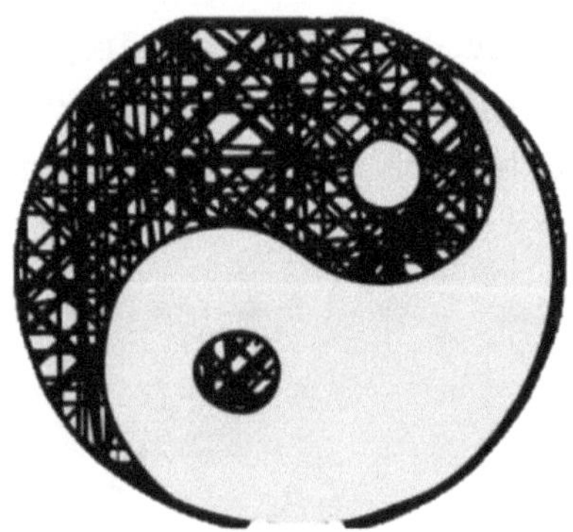

Receiving:

If somehow you reach the final phase of manifestation, are you resonating with the outcome you are excited about? What is Resonating – process? Let's talk about a person named "Mr. A", who has a bank balance of 100 Cr. That person knowingly or unknowingly creates a vibration surrounding his body. If you meet him, you can get those vibes of 100Cr from him through the way he talks, behaves, walks, relaxes, and comforts that he is enjoying. So, Mr. A is under a "specific vibration"; let's consider the name of that vibration is "XYZ".

Let's discuss another person, Mr. B, who has only Rs 100 in his bank account. His current vibration is "xyz." We can all see the difference in his vibration.

If Mr. B wants to work upon his vibration and resonate with the other rich vibration, he has to start first from the 1st phase of the manifestation, then the 2nd and finally come to the 3rd. In 3rd phase, he has to act as if he has 100 CR in his account and resonates with the activities of MR. A is doing. When You resonate, you virtually connect with the other's vibration and attract what is currently on the virtual level.

In Asking, Believing and Resonating the vibration, you start deserving what you want, and when you deserve, you get. If you have been following these 3 phases just as it is, either you have got what you wanted or are already in the process of getting the same. There is no way Manifestation fails. Failing is impossible in this process if three Manifestation processes are rightly followed.

Is the "Law of Attraction" the same as Manifestation?

The answer is "Yes".

The manifestation process is not new. Many great people have applied this The 3-phase technique conquered the world, won many hearts, and earned money gargantuanly. Hence, few gave rise to a new nomenclature for this process - Manifestation. Some named "Law of attraction, some named "Law of Synchronicity", some named "Sowing & Reaping", some named Cause & Effect, etc. But the matter of fact is – This is Manifestation. What we want, we manifest, be it constructively or destructively. We do manifest. So, beware of what you are manifesting knowingly or unknowingly.

RULE 10: MINDFUL - VALUE SLEEP

Sleep is always underrated. Since birth, we have thought "Sleeping" is automatic; we welcome "sleep" every night. But Sleep is self-driven, not auto-driven. During nighttime, some sleep at 9 pm, some sleep at 10 pm, some at 11 pm, and some might go beyond midnight.

So, what is the best time? What is the minimum sleep time we should follow? Should we sleep in the afternoon? What if we don't sleep at night and do it during the morning? What happens when we don't sleep? Many such questions might be popping up inside your mind. Or maybe you are thinking, "How does it affect our self-image or dignity?"

As I already shared with you, my condition during 2020 when I was almost deprived of sleep. I remember those days. Every day, I used to have a self-tortured night. I was living the life of a living dead man. If I recapitulate my days before 2020, I never emphasized "sleep". It was always my unconscious decision to sleep. I used to sleep at 2 pm or 3 pm, sometimes 4 pm. I never realized what I was doing those days until anxiety attacks hit me hard. I am not saying that the same thing will happen to everyone, but why take risks?

Always remember that if sleep is compromised, our health gets compromised, and if health takes a toll, our self-image can't be high or positive. In my case, irrespective of my knowledge, skills and successes I started having in my life, everything went for a toss when my health deteriorated. That day, I realized good health = healthy sleep + healthy eating.

In our regular lives, our sleep has its cycles, and every cycle takes 90 minutes to complete. For a normal human being, five cycles are considered to be healthy. Less than five or more five cycles could be a little unhealthy.

If five cycles are considered normal and healthy sleep, 5 cycles X 90 minutes = 450 minutes; 7 hours of 30-minute sleep is healthy. Are you getting 7 hours 30 minutes of sleep every day? Now, you might be using your brain thinking, "Can we bifurcate these five cycles into two halves?

For instance, can this way be the ideal for one cycle in the afternoon and four cycles at night? Logically, this can be the last way, but it is not ideal. The last way is because the required five cycles are completed, but why is this not ideal? Think of the time when technical evolution was not even thought of. We used to live in the jungles or used to live in the woody or muddy huts. There was no technology, lights, mobiles, or fans; we were living a natural life. The life is what our universe might have thought of. The universe did not create technology. So, to return to the topic, suppose no light bulb has been created yet, and we are sleeping at night. In response to darkness, the brain produces a hormone called Melatonin. Melatonin helps with the timing of our circadian rhythms (Internal clock). If the internal clock is disturbed, our health will be disturbed.

Many of us knowingly or unknowingly mess with our internal clocks, which leads to many physical illnesses and diseases. We live in an advanced technological Universe with mobiles, laptops, TVs, etc. Before we go to sleep, we only use these gadgets. These gadgets mess with our sleep cycles, negatively affecting melatonin secretion.

Now, the answer to your "bifurcated sleep" is why this is not ideal. A shocking truth about Melatonin secretion is that it is blocked when someone is exposed to light. During the afternoon, there is light and low-frequency Melatonin secretion, which indirectly affects our sleep. The next reason why afternoon sleep is not ideal is that if we are career-oriented, then using afternoon time professionally is more important than sleeping. Isn't that healthy for our careers? Sleeping during the afternoon is indirectly sucking hours from our professional lives. So, think again and again. If you do night shifts and don't sleep at night, that's a different case. Anyway, that also hurts your melatonin secretion. Still, when you change your internal clock, your body starts going to the automaticity point and gets accustomed to your new schedule.

Lack of sleep hours or cycles is a life threat. Beware of it. If not taken care of, a lack of healthy sleep might strike you one day. This is not only my wisdom; my real-life experience has taught me the importance of sleep.

Although if you are doing meditation, you can somewhat compensate for the losses of the sleep cycle, no doubt, but try not to game with sleep. Practice Mindful-Value Sleeping.

RULE 11: MINDFUL-VALUE EATING

Like mindful value sleep, mindfulness during eating or drinking also matters the most to your health. Again, health comes into the picture. We can't play easy with our health; killing health is killing ourselves. We need to respect our bodies. Just be a little mindful of what you are eating or drinking. A person who respects self, loves self, and always stands for self will never mess with health.

Every serving that goes inside your body will impact it constructively or destructively. It has to be seen, heard and felt inside. Every serving goes inside our body, reciprocating with either "Thank you" or "Hate you." What does your food reciprocate from inside? Sometimes, we listen to our tongue's message and prioritize taste over health. If you eat badly, your stomach cries in pain. When your stomach is not happy, how can you be happy?

As mentioned earlier too, good health = healthy sleep + healthy eating. Anytime you mess with your sleep or eating habits, you will surely face the consequences. Nowadays, people are not dying of eating less but eating more. With a disturbed stomach and incomplete sleep cycles, you can't dare to dream of a heroic life but a weak - disturbed life. The choice is yours because life is yours.

11/ 90 / 90 FORMULA – READINESS CHECKING …
(Tick the box if you are ready to start)

11 – I accept these 11 Rules are important for my dignified life

90– I execute 90-minute daily on these 11 Rules without fail

90– I am committed to following 11 Rules daily for 90 mins. for the next
    90 days.

Value System 3 – POSITIVITY

Have you ever said to someone, "Just be positive, yaar!" or has anyone told you the same? Is it easy to be positive when experiencing difficulties or your worst times? Is Positivity a hype or a hope?

I still remember my days in the bank, but I was not so motivated to work. I was trying my heart and soul to get a better opportunity in the banking sector. Then I came across Government Bank's Recruitment, a written test, and an interview. Although I knew cracking a written test would not be easy, I appeared, and believe it or not, I cracked it. I was super happy and excited.

During those days, I worked at a private bank in Delhi. When I got this news, I was thrilled. Then I saw the interview date was very near, and I had to return to Kolkata to appear for that interview. I sent my boss a leave request, and he rejected it. My condition was so mixed; I was happy to get selected, but at the same time, I was dead angry at my boss. Anyway, I didn't want to miss this opportunity and was sure I would also crack the Interview. And finally, I did what my heart said: I resigned from the job. Imagine my situation; I resigned from a well-established job in a private bank to get into a government bank even before appearing for the interview. This was my sheer overconfidence.

Anyway, I came back to Kolkata and finally attended the Interview. I still remember the day I visited the Bank's main building where the interview was scheduled. Finally, I appeared, and I failed the interview. Did you hear, "I failed the interview? " Yes, you heard it right. I failed. Not only did I fail the interview, but I also failed in my existing job, which I resigned from because I was overconfident. I failed my confidence level. I failed at that amazing opportunity, which could have changed my life. I was shattered, and I wanted to cry. But how to cry? I told you I was an introvert. I was scared of crying in front of everyone.

I decided to walk almost 14 km to my house from the interview location because I wanted to cry. I wanted to cry, shout, and even ask God many questions while looking at the sky, and I did. Even though I didn't realize it, I walked almost 14 km, crying, shouting, and asking reactive questions.

If you had been there and asked me, "Are you alright?" I would have answered with three words: "I am finished!"

Many things happen; we are broke, shattered, and almost lost. We have no motivation, no YouTube channel, or reading books relieves us. Every positive thing seems to be fake, bogus, and a waste. Even our self-image touches the bottom negatively. We believe "luck is more important than work" or "luck doesn't favour me."

So, you realize, if you are broke, can you speak any language effectively?

If you are upset or hopeless, can you communicate effectively?

If you feel lost, can your talk motivate others?

If you feel unlucky or unhappy, can you talk positively to anyone?

You know the answer, right?

So, what's the solution to this Positive Attitude, especially during difficult times?

Before I answer this question, I would like to tell you what I think about those difficult times, especially the bank's interview case I shared with you. If you ask me how I feel now about that bank interview case after so many years gone by, my answer would be in six words, "Thank God! I was not selected". Yes, this is what I feel now. Now, I am a coach with a team of almost 200+ coaches. I love it. I am unsure if my earnings would be better if I were in a bank now, but when I credit salaries to my coaches' account, I feel blessed. At least my decision and my difficult past created an amazing heroic plan for me. I am earning and making a difference in people's lives. I want to scream and say, "Thank you for my difficult times; you made my life".

Someone said it right: "When our plan succeeds, we feel good, but when we don't get what we plan, the plan must be from the superpower, and he is the best at his job. We must surrender to him but never question him."

For a Positive life, 10 things never forget;

1. Focus on the Present: there is no negative in the present situation
   (All negatives lie in the past and future; change your focus)

2. Believe in God's plan
   (Believe it or not, whatever happens, happens for the best)

3. Self-love brings positive thinking
   (Raise your dignity level, Refrain from all the stimuli which negatively affect self)

4. Love your work
   (Choose the work that is progressive, great serving to society and loving to self)

5. Set meaningful goals in life
   (Goal provides clarity, motive, sense of glory and good spirits in the process)

6. Positive Visualization
   (Close your eyes and visualize positive past moments & Create desired future moments)

7. Positive Affirmation
   (Focus on positive self-talk and attract desired future with RAS)

8. Use Right Brain Activities
   (Go spiritual places / meet childhood friends / visit birth place / dance & singing / art & craft / spend time in hobbies / go solo movies and travel / backwards walking etc.)

9. Practice mindfulness
    (Live your every second mindfully / Focus on deep breaths / focus on visuals, sounds and feelings which often get ignored)

10. Create Positive Proximity
    (Positivity attracts positivity. Spend time with people who are positive, progressive and proactive, always ready for the action)

Value System 4 – EMPATHY

One easy question: You may laugh or wonder, "Why am I asking this silly question?" but the answer could be a million dollars.

Have you ever cried watching emotional movies or serials? If the answer is "No," that's fine. But if the answer is "Yes," we need to talk.

You have empathy if you feel emotion and tears come out of your eyes while watching movies or serials or listening to anyone's emotional situation. If you can cry or feel emotional even when you know that the movie or serial is not real, this requires a lot of softness in your heart. It is 100% true!

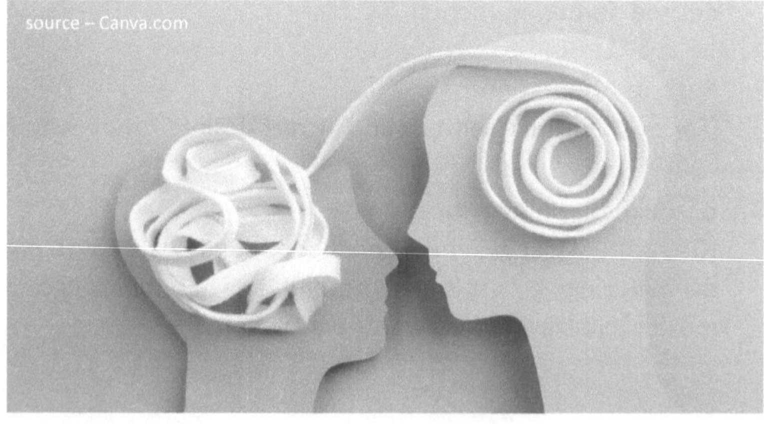

Empathy is one of the most important qualities of a successful person. This justification does not mean that those who don't cry or feel emotional don't have empathy; they can even have it. But the question is, if they have emotion, why don't they show it? Is there any issue with sharing their own emotions?

Why don't some people feel someone's pain? What about those who want to cry but feel' "crying is a weakness"? What do you think? Is crying a weakness? Let me clear the air; you can go outside your house and start smiling or laughing; it's easy, but can you go outside and cry? Not so easy, right? So crying is difficult. Then it is proven that "crying is not a weakness". Anything difficult, weak people can't attempt that. So, next time you feel like crying, cry and share your emotions because crying shows emotional honesty and only strong people can cry.

Inside the organization,

Can a manager cry when his situations are difficult?

- If they feel, then why not?

Can a senior manager cry when they feel emotion?

- Yes, they should!

Can an AVP or VP cry when they feel broke?

- Yes, For sure!

Can a C.E.O. cry when they can't handle their mental pressure?

- Yes! Yes! Yes!

Then why do most corporate leaders feel ashamed of crying? Why do they suppress their emotions until they finally outburst?

Empathy is feeling someone's pain and making efforts to heal that pain. Please do not get jumbled with the word "Sympathy" here. Sympathy pertains to considering someone's pain and understanding that we might not try to heal it if someone has pain. There is another word called "apathy," which means no interest in anything or anyone. People with apathy are living dead; their contribution to human relationships is BIG ZERO.

Empathetic listening came from empathy only. When you give your heart and soul to listen to and understand someone's pain, yes, that is empathy. No empathy, no listening, because when we listen with empathy, we don't only listen to what is being said, but also what is not being said or maybe what message comes out of their body- language. When we empathize while listening to someone, we make many positive changes in our body language.

For instance, to listen effectively, we should lean toward the speaker, maintain eye contact, nod while listening, and adjust our body language. If we don't see our speaker, we are probably not listening to him.

Empathetic Listening is the key; it connects both you and me… When people speak from the heart, their language melts with their colourful emotions. Just hearing them for the sake of hearing means understanding their language only, not the colours, not the emotions, or, as we can say, "not the actual message." So, simple hearing is no longer an option.

Those who have empathy know what emotion is.

Those who know what emotion is know how to deal with it.

Those who know how to deal with it, know how not to hurt it, and

Those who don't hurt it actually make it! Yes!

They make it to effective communication.

They make it to impressive relation and finally…

They make it to progressive realization.

Value System 5 – HUMILITY

Humility is one of the most outstanding mental qualities. It means to be simple, grounded and down to earth. It is very easy to think powerful even if we are not powerful, but it is special and rare when a powerful person does not show off his power and remains grounded.

What do you call a successful person who shows people his power?

What do you call a person who is successful and dominating others who are under?

What do you call a person using foul language in front of others?

What do you call a person who is demeaning others and making people feel small?

What do you call a person who knows he is wrong but still counting other's mistakes?

What do you call a person who is wrongly using his positional power (designation-wise)?

What do you call a person who performs well but doesn't follow his boss's instructions?

What do you call a person who physically hit and hurt a person to get importance?

What do you call a person who says to his people, "I know everything, don't teach me"?

These people are arrogant! Some are knowingly arrogant, and some are unaware of it. So, it is recommended that people be alert and check their arrogance level regularly.

Are these people anti-social? – No!

Are these people unaware of what is right or what is wrong? – No!

Are these people qualified? – Chances are high!

Are these people from a good family background? – Yes, no doubt!

Are these people knowingly being arrogant? – Maybe not aware of it!

Why do some people knowingly become arrogant?

Arrogance makes them feel powerful.

Arrogance makes them feel special.

Arrogance makes them feel pampered.

Arrogance makes them feel – unique and numero-uno (No. 1)

Arrogance makes them feel irreplaceable.

Arrogance makes them feel like the boss.

In short, some people feel power comes when people are scared of them, but the reality is that "Power comes when you serve others to be happy, lucky, and progressive." Think about this important statement, and read it again and again!

If someone is arrogant, he will never want others to be happier than him, or if he finds someone, he might generate jealousy or anger.

If someone is arrogant, she will never want others to be luckier than her, and if she finds someone, she might plan something atrocious against them.

If someone is arrogant, he will never want others to be more progressive than him, or in case he finds someone, he might try to affect that person negatively.

Arrogance, egotism, or a sense of superiority do no good to anyone. Instead, they provoke anger, jealousy, irritation, resentment, and outrage. In short, arrogance sabotages people internally. An arrogant person may dominate people initially for a short time but can't stop or create a hindrance to anyone's success path who is really deserving. So, we can say, "Arrogant might win the start and prove, but loses every next move" because internal damages are more excruciating than external damages.

The time has come to forgive ourselves for our arrogant feelings. Sometimes we don't understand what we do. Sometimes, our competitive mindset arouses arrogance inside us. The time has come to beautify the world and make it best to live for others to come. Some are ahead, some are behind, but we all are moving. We all will get our share to enjoy. Life has enough for all; no one can empty the ocean. We need to focus on progressing and helping others to progress.

If you imagine an arrogant person, will you feel at peace talking to him? Now, imagine someone who is so down to earth, humble, and always thinks about everyone's success and his success. Now think how peacefully and beautifully that person will talk to you.

Humility touches the heart, catches the eyes and galvanizes the progress. Where Arrogance stops the conversation, hurts the heart and damages the self. So, it's our life, our choice. We make it to humility or break it to arrogance.

People who practice humility talk less, but everyone listens and feels at peace when they talk. According to people who practice humility, "Communication is a continuous process, but that doesn't mean talking continuously. Even without speaking, we can speak many things through our bodies. So, always improve the silence when communicating vocally or through your body. There is no use of talking if silence is peaceful and progressive." Read this paragraph for the best insight into communication.

Our communication should not break the silence but rather improve the silence.

It's so strange! The previous statement resonates with humility, while Arrogant people always try to break the silence and get noticed.

The more you go big and gargantuan, the simpler and more approachable you must be. This gives peace and happiness. People who have humility are second to God-like status, rarely found. Why are they God-like? They are because they are powerful, great servers, change agents, and down to earth. Engraving humility inside us will make us soft but protected. Soft people are better communicators. Soft is just like "birth of a child"; when you touch, you feel soft. So, soft represents life. Then what is hard?

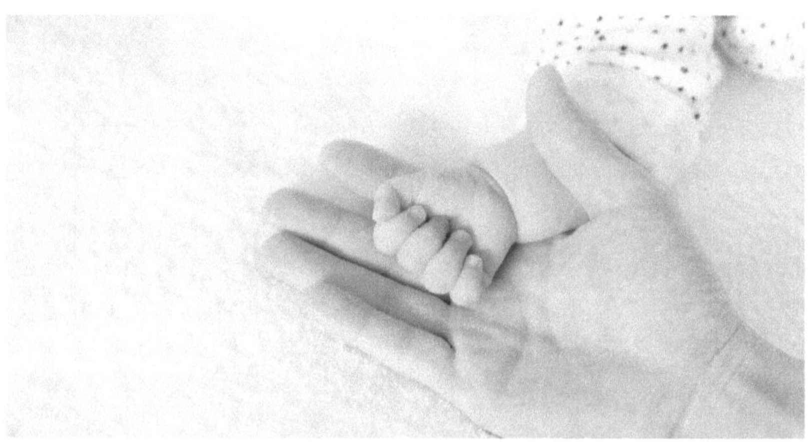

Have you ever touched a dead body? It's hard.
So, hard represents death.

Never forget that "Soft represents life".

Some say, "Others will hurt people who are soft".
This is also true, but did you notice what I mentioned above

- "Soft but Protected"

Here, "protected" means maintaining Integrity and dignity. These two values make us powerful, while Empathy and humility make us soft. Powerful people create better lives for others, while soft people create valuable relationships for others.

If you are soft but not protected with Integrity and Dignity, people will take you for granted and consider you soft. They will dominate you and keep you busy pleasing them. If you are soft, you might abandon all your priorities and start giving up your precious time, gaining a relationship but losing your own life. When you are Powerful and Soft – you create a Heroic Future for yourself.

Our current challenge is,

We have "Powerfuls" who are not Likable (soft).

We have "Likables" who are not powerful.

If anyone can decode the balance code, they will rise and shine in a heroic life. The universe will personally manifest everything for that person.

Whatever that person speaks, others will be pleased to listen to it.

It will seem like life will be set right, and the total impression will be tight.

Truth - 8
YOU ARE SELLING TRUST,
NOT JUST A WORD

Do you love to sell? Most people don't like to sell. Some are in pain because they are still inside sales jobs, even if they dislike selling. This means most people hate sales jobs but still do it forcibly. Why so much negative feeling against Sales jobs, where Sales jobs are the best, and people who sell create more money for themselves?

BELIEVE IT OR NOT, EVERYONE SELLS!

YES! This is true. We all are selling directly or indirectly. How?

Have you ever tried to convince anyone? No doubt, yes!

For instance, a son convinces his father to go on a short trip with his friends. A daughter is trying to convince her mother to go for a sleepover at her friend's house. A wife is trying to convince her husband with amazing culinary talents. A husband tries to convince his wife by going to malls and buying something special for her. Are these not sales?

If you see these situations literally, you might not feel this, but the question is, why is person A trying to convince person B? The answer is very simple: Person A has an idea and wants to sell it to Person B. This selling requires conviction, and conviction requires communication.

How do you convince people with conviction?

What is the difference between confidence and conviction? Confidence is about self. We feel confident when we know ourselves well and have the right knowledge and skills to serve others. In short, we trust ourselves and our talents. But Conviction comes when others start believing in our knowledge and skills. When we are confident and speak to get the audience's trust, we need to speak with conviction. Conviction needs power, and power comes from three components:

1. Speak with Integrity

2. Speak with Powerful body language

3. Speak with Power Voice

Speak with Integrity is powerful:

Knowing you are right, your ways are right, and you are speaking for the right outcome or results will boost your conviction level and speak with power. With conviction, you become like Arjuna from Mahabharata. When Arjuna was facing his own people on the battlefield, he was already shattered and about to quit, but his master Krishna helped him ignite "Integrity Inside" Arjuna.

Finally, Arjuna fought right, spoke right, and felt right. Though many people might disagree with Krishna and Arjuna's values, integrity won. Integrity always wins, so those who speak with Integrity win every person, every heart, and every talk.

Speaking with integrity says to speak to improve, make solutions, speak to progress, make things better, get the right results, speak to get peace, and speak to be happy.

What else do you want more from Integrity? It has answers to every problem in life. Imagine you are angry with somebody, you are going to say something bad to her, you are going to hit him hard, then you realize "Integrity".

"Integrity" won't allow you to remain angry or throw bad words or actions at others. Integrity will always help you speak solution, not problem.

Speak with Powerful Body Language:

This means that when you speak with integrity, your body language will also help you gain the trust of others. As the saying goes, "People may speak with manipulations, but body language says it all."

Experts say body language is 55% efficient, so use your whole body when speaking. When people lie, they can't synch their words with their facial expressions, hands, eyes, etc., so they neither sound nor seem confident. Hence, their conviction level is zero.

Right Talk will always promote Right Action, which will always be reflected in your Power Body Language. So next time you speak with conviction, **LOOK** at the listener while speaking with a mild **SMILE** on your face. Be it standing or sitting posture, a slight **LEANING FORWARD** to the speaker would help the speaker lead the conversation.

Speaking with both **OPEN HANDS** near the shoulder area will produce more clarity in the words. Also, listening to the listener **NODDING** would help you get both attention and trust.

Speak with the Power voice:

It means to speak louder when you are confident. When people are not confident, their voice quality deteriorates, slows down, stumbles, and is often inaudible. Voice complements the word. It is right to speak politely, and the same can be practised.

When something goes wrong, we must speak up loudly and not rudely. We may sound like we don't like it or are angry, but this is all shown in our voices, not inside our heads.

If I dislike something or feel I need to shout, I will do so to show my power, but I will not be rude. I will shout with a powerful voice and body language, but the language will be assertive. Here, assertive means controlled, loud, and respectable.

I still remember what happened to me as a banker, in 2008.

I used to work at a private limited bank in Kolkata. One unfortunate morning, I was talking to one of my colleagues, Raj, outside the bank campus. Suddenly, we saw on the street a girl got down from the bike, waited for some time and then a car came from nowhere. she got into that car and then left. The whole incident was so random and fast; it just happened. Raj and I had a glance the same. We looked at each other and shrugged our shoulders with little surprising expressions on our faces. That incident was not that special, but yes, that created a little humour for both of us. We finally got inside the bank and started working on our daily accountabilities. Raj used to be sitting beside me.

I still remember that day, before our working hours started, Raj and I were discussing the same girl on the street as a fun topic. While talking, one of the female colleagues, Sangita, felt we were talking about her. Sangita went to our Branch Manager and made a complaint against us. Raj and I were called. The branch manager threatened both of us not to repeat the same. Raj was silent, and I was crying a lot. I was not crying because my BM was scolding me, but I knew the intensity of the topic.

The topic was so shameful for me, and I am not a guy to take this on my self-respect. Even I knew my BM was doing his job. But I knew I didn't deserve that.

I wish I knew what conviction was that day. I wish I knew what integrity is that day. I wish I could have used my powerful body language and voice that day. But I couldn't. I wasn't wrong that day, and I was punished. My BM's scolding was not the real punishment to me. What hurt me was that I could have stood up for my self-respect that day, but I didn't. My BM didn't punish me that day, but I did to myself.

If today were the same day, I would have never cried but surely spoke with conviction to my BM: "Sir, we both are innocent; if this girl continues making wrong allegations about us, we will simply go to HR and file a complaint against her. Without knowing the truth, Sir, you can't blame us. Yes, sir, you can question us, but you can't hold both of us liable for something we have not done."

My Power talk could have convinced my boss that day or not, that is secondary. What is primary is that if that day I could speak with conviction, I could stand for myself and save my self-respect, I would have felt better and relieved. Anyway, I forgave myself for not protecting my dignity. I forgave myself because my self-image was at risk. Believe me, even I had forgiven that girl who misunderstood us and my BM who shouted at us without knowing the truth.

If I can forgive myself for my mistakes that day (I didn't stand up for my self-respect), I must forgive everyone. So, my story could give you a little idea about what could happen if we lack conviction.

Conviction doesn't give us ultimate glory but provides self-reliance and respect. Conviction makes us powerful. Conviction heals us to believe in self. We may not win every time with conviction, but we win ourselves with conviction every time we practise.

I have one question: What should you do if people doubt you, blame you for no reason or say all the wrong things about you? Would you speak up or keep your mouth shut?

I said this earlier, also speaking right to improve the situation. But you must speak up when questioned, blamed, or doubted. Conviction never fails; rather, it brings hope to others. Students often come to me with low confidence and not-so-good English, and finally, after a few sessions only, they understand their mistakes. The majority focus on language, part of the outside locus of control. Still, conviction focuses on the inside locus of control, i.e. right speaking, right body language and the right voice, and speaking with Integrity.

When you focus on the inside locus of control, the outside locus of control will be handled easily. Focus on speaking correctly; even if people don't show they believe you, one day, they will. They will know that you are right.

Focus on using body language while speaking because often, right doesn't sound right when not supported by powerful gestures and eye contact. Body language galvanizes conviction into reality and helps us build trust.

Speak less Impress More

A soft speaker is good, but soft people often can't speak hard when needed. Sometimes, speaking hard really matters the truth to bring to the table. Speaking hard doesn't mean becoming rude, but taking the voice pitch slightly on a higher side with modulation but keeping the listener's respect.

People who always speak more and use high-pitch while speaking most of the time are often taken lightly by others. On the contrary, people who are always polite but suddenly something happens, and that person starts speaking in high pitch; others can't take that lightly, so his high pitch is taken seriously, and his talk is noticed and heard.

Again, speak less, but speak right!

Speak Politely always, but when blamed for no reason, speak with fire and burn the nonsense created around you.

Speak rightly and politely, even if others anger you for no reason.

Speak rightly, even if you do not like that person.

Speak right when others see no solutions.

Speak right when others demean you.

Speak right when others need you.

Speak right when you want to say "No!" to others

Speak right, even if you hate the person.

When you sow right, you reap right! This is inevitable!

Next time, when you want to impress someone, focus on three things: speak right, speak rightly with powerful body language and a powerful voice. Speak louder but not rudely. You may speak with high pitch but do not dominate others.

Right Selling comes from the Right presentation with the right intention. You may fail the presentation, but keep your right intention intact with Integrity. Don't fail with the right intentions. The right intentions give rise to Conviction.

Next time the word" Sales" comes up, respect it. Sales are the backbone of any industry. Sales must occur, or else any industry will die. Likewise, we sell our thoughts, ideas, emotions, and feelings to others. So, "Sales" is never wrong. However, seeing "Sales" with a demeaning attitude is wrong. Mind this!

To be all set to sell, respect "Sales"!
When we respect, we will be close to perfect (in sales).

Sales help us serve and help others progress. Without serving and helping intention, we can't sell. We can't sell just anything for money if companies sell high-ticket products with low-value proposition products. This is simply an injustice; this is hurting the customers' trust.

Here, customers mean anyone receiving something from us physically or emotionally.

So next time you sell, do not hate sales; ensure you sell right! Conviction comes to the right people, who speak and serve right.

If you are selling somebody guaranteed success, will you feel bad?

If you sell a Heroic personality to someone, will you feel bad?

If you sell Guaranteed Lifetime Smile to anyone, will you feel bad?

If you are selling someone his dream life, will you feel bad?

If your answer is "No, " Sell hard, but talk soft!

Don't think about people's opinions about you. When the intention is to serve and help, money is just the byproduct. Sell right! Sell with power! Sell with Integrity! Sell with Conviction!

Truth - 9

D - ELEPHANT'S FEAR OF LION

Are elephants scared of lions? Are elephants less powerful than lions? Are elephants inferior to lions? Are elephants less intelligent than lions?

Do elephants not deserve to be the king of the jungle? What do you think?

Many questions, but one answer – "No!"

Elephants are larger than lions, heavier than lions, and even more humble than lions. As far as "fear" is concerned, elephants are not scared of lions. Due to their size and strength, healthy elephants could fend off a lion easily.

Then why do the majority have a notion that lions can beat elephants? Is that a "general perception" conditioned inside the majority for a long time?

Let's talk about people who fear their bosses and any higher authority. Many times, it is seen that we speak impressively well with our level people or people who are our subordinates. But when it comes to speaking in front of ~~the lions~~, oh sorry, bosses, we feel discomfort and nervousness. Actually why? Do bosses have more intelligence than us? Or do we feel they are more powerful? Or we might feel they can influence our progress inside the organization. Maybe the last statement makes some sense to you, right?

You know adult elephants are not exactly scared of lions, even though you have rarely heard that "a lion hunted an elephant" seldomly happened. Exceptions are always there, but exceptions can't be taken as examples. Yes, you can say the presence of lions could make elephants nervous, not scared. Elephants especially become nervous about protecting their young calves, as lions are one of the few predators that can potentially harm those young, sometimes injured or isolated elephants.

Employees are often scared of bosses or higher authority because they fear losing their jobs, positions or increments. Likewise, elephants are scared of losing their calves when the pride of lions encircles them to attack. At least employees are at lesser risk; they are not losing their lives, ha ha ha...jokes apart.

When a position comes, power comes; the person with power often shows power to their subordinates. Sometimes, power is imposed with humility and care, but most of the time, it gets into people's brains, and they forget right and wrong. So, this statement is very important or could be an important insight into understanding your boss or any higher authority.

For instance, if your boss humbly imposes power, he will care for you and want a good and progressive career. But on the contrary, if you see your boss imposing power with arrogance, that means even if you show respect to him, you can't progress in that organization.

Arrogant bosses would always want their subordinates to work under him only. So, in the first case, you are working not with fear but with care. Yes, when your upline, boss, or higher authority wants your progress and tries to understand you, you would also show gratitude to them and work your best. But in the second case, when your upline is dominating you, there is no progress you can expect from your higher authority.

So, one more important thing here is to work beyond your salary. You have work and quality standards, plus integrity, so even if you are unhappy with your current salary. Suppose you feel you deserve better than your current salary. In that case, it's ok to explore the market for better opportunities, but until you get any new opportunity, do not downgrade your work standards just because you are not happy at your current job for any damn reason. You can't select your boss, but you can select your work standard.

First, ensure you maintain your work standards and integrity. Correct your side first, then move on to the next challenge: dealing with your boss or higher authority.

In my organization, I am the CEO, and all my employees (90% coaches) can approach me anytime; this liberty has been given to everyone, but yes, we follow an organizational hierarchy system, and everyone follows it.

I have been so approachable to everyone. Now, the question is, are my employees scared of me? Can't they speak to me freely? Should they feel nervous when I am around? My expected answer would be "No!" I would never want my employees to feel nervous around me, and I would never be bossy or dominating.

Anyway, I know one thing: if my employees are scared or feel dominated, they will never give their best. I believe every coach and employee of my organization has that freedom. They know their accountabilities and must follow the work process and deliver. They can approach me anytime for any suggestions.

Regarding working culture, I believe in a Dignity-intact work standard, where every employee feels the taste of self-respect working in the organization. Self-respect always beats salary satisfaction. Salary is undoubtedly a big motivator, and this motivation makes people happy. But imagine you are losing respect from your higher authority, or you are not enjoying your work. You are always being transferred from one place to another without genuine reason. How far can you expect your tenure with that organization to go, even if you get your desired salary?

This chapter is titled "D-Elephant's Fear of Lion"; here, "D" stands for Dignity. The dignity of an elephant matters. Whether an employee or an elephant, dignity is the primary prerequisite for living within society. In simpler terms, dignity means self-respect. If I possess the necessary knowledge and skills for my current job and give my all to my organization, there is no reason to fear my boss or any higher authorities. Fear arises when there is a disconnect between my accountabilities and responsibilities and my performance level. Fear occurs when my contributions do not meet my company's standards.

Fear comes when I know I am not happily working and giving my full potential. Fear comes when I know there is an integrity issue from my end. So, if I feel shy or reluctant in front of my top-level officials, I need to work on my Integrity and Dignity.

When I am right, I work right, I perform my daily accountabilities, for which I am answerable, and I do it at my best level with my best knowledge and skills. If I am doing this, there is no way I would be scared of my bosses or upline. Through my high work standards, I do not give any chance to my higher authorities to speak against me or to have any doubt about my skills. So, whenever I face them, my head will be upright high with a mild smile, and my eyes connect to their eyes with so much warmth. When there is warmth in our eyes, respect will be intact for the next person.

So, next time you face ~~the lions,~~ oh sorry again, your higher authority, project warmth towards them, but please don't expect the same from them. If you see, then your luck. But yes, you can only help yourselves. So next time, see the up-levels with warmth and talk with power so they can even feel that power inside you. If you are right, there is no way you feel dominated. But you can't question your boss's humility or humiliation if you do not give your best at work.

Mind it! Keep your head high and upright, smile in front of every person you encounter, and maintain a high work standard and dignity. Believe me, the rest will be taken care of.

One important suggestion is never to outshine your boss or higher authority. You can always be assertive toward your boss but never try to make him feel you are smarter than him.

If your boss speaks more, pay attention, lean forward, and listen to him or her; nod your head while listening. Become genuinely interested in listening to him or her. If your boss speaks less, that means your boss has good insight, which can help you progress. So, ask more questions regarding work, strengths, and weaknesses. Your boss would like it. Ensure you do it genuinely, not just for the sake of doing it.

10 impressive ways to communicate with your bosses / higher authority:

1. Start with small stuff   – Hello, ma'am! / How are you ma'am?

2. Be specific when you talk – Know exactly what you need from her.

3. Say No for the right reason – Say no politely if the boss's wants are ethically wrong.

4. Connect with Value System   – Say to yourself, "If I am right, I don't need to be scared of anyone?"

5. Boss is not a robot   – Try to understand her; even the boss may have difficulties.

6. Speak as an ally, not an enemy   – Don't forget, you both share the same goal.

7. Raise your hand and speak up   – Be the first to speak up, participate and get noticed.

8. Personalized feedback   – Always request and act from the boss.

9. Be Accountable   – Be the CEO of your work and take the blame constructively.

10. Ask for Mentorship   – Ask for knowledge and skill training to progress inside the org.

No one cares what your inside story or intentions are because what you do, you show, and the world only creates an impression out of that. So, if next time your inner self asks you to speak to your boss and says, "Is it important to speak to my boss now? Will she take it wrongly?" before you even get any answer, go to her and ask, "How are you ma'am? Is everything fine?".

Always talk to yourself and galvanize yourself to the next level, especially when you feel shy. Remember these two lines, "There is nothing wrong in doing the right thing, and there is never a wrong time to do the right thing."

So, let the elephant be a little nervous while saving the calves. There is nothing wrong with the elephant feeling alert, ready, and respectful of the lion—the lion deserves it. Anyway, the Lion is the king of the jungle.

It's the same with you, too. Showing respect to the higher authorities and feeling a little nervous in front of them is part of the game, but humans are a little more privileged because. In the jungle, elephants will never become lions, whatever it takes. Even elephants get self-realization; lions will be lions, and elephants will never become lions.

But elephants can surely be transformed into lions in the jungle of humans. In corporate life, any employee's position will not be the same in the future; It will change, considering the employee's integrity, hard work, and right brain during his work. It might take a little time or a lot of time. Still, if an employee is deserving, knowledgeable, skilled, assertive, and has the conviction to speak, any employee can get the leadership role and become a lion.

This chapter doesn't discuss how to be a boss or a leader because even if you become a boss or any leader at any top level, there will always be someone positioned higher than you. So, focus on your upward communication style with leaders. You are not a servant of your boss; you are your boss's right or left hand. Without a left or right hand, even your boss is helpless.

So, if you are right, keep flying your kite (work) in the sky (progress), keep the kite going higher and higher (generate more revenues) and touch the stars (get noticed and recognized). Now, once your kite touches the sky, everyone will talk about you, the kite and the sky only; no one will talk about whether you spoke or not while flying the kite.

When you are a performer, your work impresses your boss more than your talk. So, focus on work and speak less. Ensure your personality reflects 5 Super TQPS Values - Integrity, Dignity, Empathy, Positivity, and Humility.

Truth - 10

FLIRT WITH YOUR RIGHT BRAIN

What is flirting? Is flirting healthy? How can we flirt with our own brains?

Flirting has a literal meaning: You find someone attractive but are not serious about a relationship. So, flirting is always healthy and fun.

Are you left-handed or right-handed? The chances are very high that you are right-handed. Am I right? But why is the majority of us right-handed? Or might our parents have conditioned us to use our right hand more? Can this be true? Reasons could be anything, but knowingly or unknowingly, we have ignored the true potential of our left hand. Do we use our left eye equally? Do we use our left ear equally? Do we use our left leg equally? The answer is "Yes!" Then why not both hands equally?

Look at the picture above and write 10 sentences regarding this picture in your copy. You have 10 minutes to do this. It is advisable not to see the next page before you write 10 sentences.

If suppose **"Writer A" has done the idea generation and wrote the below paragraph,**

This is a nice picture. A girl is sitting on her knees and watering the plants. She is very happy. Watering plants is very important, as they give oxygen. She is holding the water pot with her right hand and wearing gloves. This picture is black and white. Some of the plants are big, and some are small. The girl is enjoying her activity.

The above statements speak about writer A and her preferred idea-generation brain. The lines mentioned above show that writer A is logical. She wrote something she saw and didn't use any imagination while generating ideas. The writer focused on the facts shown in the picture. The writer is organized. She observed the whole picture and tried to write everything possible. She did not want to leave any information.

Now check your lines. Are your lines logical or match with writer A's paragraph? If matching, then how much - 40% matching? or 80% matching? or simply 10% matching?

Now let's take another writer – Writer B's idea generation,

Wow, what a mindful moment it is. I can see a mother feeding her children. Just giving birth is not enough, but nurturing children and making their life green with growth, happy like yellow and productive like blue is one of the important responsibilities of a mother. Imagine the love and care she gives those plants as if plants are responding, "Thank you, mother". Water, planting, and caring with positive vibrations are always progressive; if given to a plant, a plant grows; if given to humans like us, we also grow and prosper.

Now, what just happened? Writer B is flirting with his right brain and making idea generation more interesting. His lines show imagination. Writer B sees something that can't be seen through the naked eye but can be felt with an open heart. He resonates with the picture of a mother's love and the plant's growth with the children's growth. Here, writer B is more emotional and freer and doesn't care about feedback, as if he is flirting with his right brain.

Now check your lines again. Are your lines imaginative or match with writer B's paragraph? If matching, then how much is 40% matching? or 80% matching? or simply 10% matching? Or are your lines being a mix of imagination and logic? Even in this case also, what is more dominating? Logical or imaginative?

Whenever I mention the word "flirting," does it bother you and make you conscious, or does this word make this chapter interesting to read? The answer will reveal many things about you, the reader.

This is not the fight of being logical or imaginative; rather, this is the real fight of your left and right brains. Yes, now we have come back to the main topic. As per neuroscience, our brain has been divided into two: the left brain and the right brain.

Left brain people are more logical, like our previous writer A, who focused on numbers, seeing facts and data, truths, possibilities, maturity, right sequence, and reality of life; in short, focusing on something which is written or given or followed before and the same we also need to follow, as per society or parents, failing to which we will face failure, criticism, conflict etc. So, the left brain is intelligent, mature and socially accepted but a little serious, too. Why not flirt with our right brain?

The right brain focuses on imagination, colours, beauty, feelings, freedom, peace, happiness, music, dance, meeting childhood friends, and being romantic. People with this brain are more energetic and madder than logical people. They are also more hopeful and less realistic.

These people may have less money but are happier. They may also be better or more successful in their relationships, if not their money.

So, the right brain is interesting, fun and enthusiastic but a little imaginative.

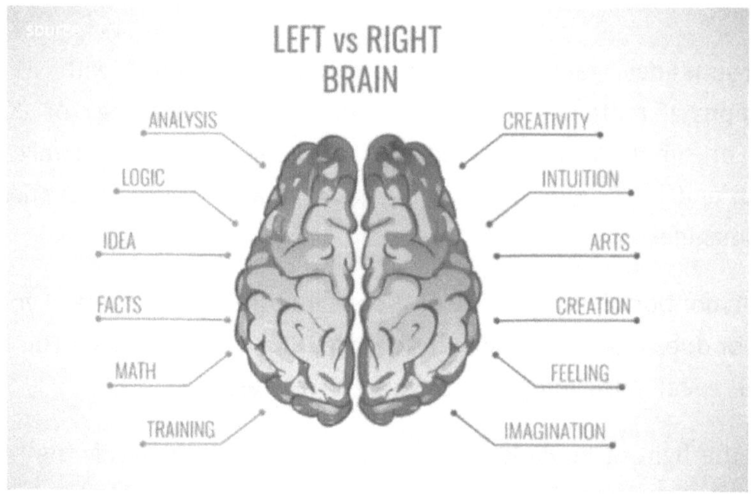

Why did I stress the fact of right-handed people and left-handed people when I started this chapter? I did that because, as per neuroscience, the right side of the body is controlled by our left brain and the left side of the body is managed by our right brain. Does that mean overuse of our right hand has triggered our left-brain power, if not totally, but partially yes?

The more we follow logic, people, theories, parents, teachers, and books, the more we become and behave like them. Nothing is wrong with that, but we have made a blunt mistake: We have ignored the power of the left hand and right brain.

As I said, there's never a wrong time to do the right thing, so we can work on our right brains now. Wow!

Here are 13 amazing Flirting hacks to activate your right brain;

1. Use left hand for small activities –

   Like holding a teacup, brushing your teeth, etc.

2. Backwards walking –

   Morning/evening exercise with backward walking with safety

3. Practice Dance forms –

   Dance to any tune; no expert steps are required; just move

4. Singing or listening to songs or playing an instrument –

   Any form of music.

5. Go Travel – Enjoy going on national and international trips, especially going alone would be adventurous (solo travelling)

6. Experiment with looks – Changing hairstyle, specs-style, dressing style, etc.

7. Enjoy the movie at the theatre alone – Enjoy the movie alone

8. Spend some time with kids of less than 8 years – be kids when with kids, play, run, jump, have fun, etc.

9. Drawing, Painting or Art & Craft – Practise DIY – activities

10. Play Games – Antakshari, Dumb-charades, Pictionary, Snake & Ladder etc.

11. Theatre & Acting – Amazing skill to improve the right brain

12. Practice meditation & mindfulness – 15 mins. everyday

13. Gardening & Watering Plants – A simple act of caring for plants will help your right brain

ARE YOU READY TO TEST YOUR BRAIN?

<u>Let's do one Right Brain Activity now:</u>

Activity:

- Take paper and pencil and be ready
- Make a square (make it a little bigger for better space)

- Try dividing it into four equal parts

Can you do this? If yes, how many pictures can you make?

1 or 2 o3, or more than 4

(do not turn the page before you answer)

Maybe you got this shown below,

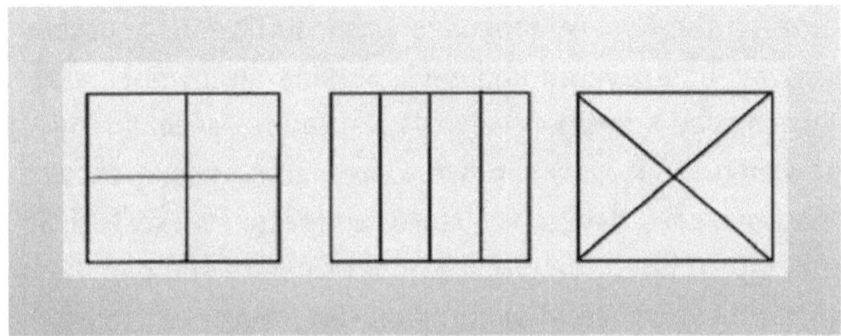

Sorry to say the above designs result from left-brain idea generation.

Could there be any more design possible with equal four parts? especially when you use your right brain. To see some more mind-boggling designs, see page no 134.

So, Right Brain Activation will always help you stand out from the crowd and be unique. Some get this from heredity, which is possible, but it can also be practised and developed.

I still remember the day I was in my post-graduation days in college. An old alumni of the same college came to our class, and our teacher introduced him as Mr. Akash and even boasted about him. We all felt so happy to see him succeed because we were also from the same college and about to graduate. So, what happened?

Someone from my class asked him, "How has been your journey to success, Mr. Akash?' and then he started,

"It has been really difficult. The initial 5 years were struggling and torturing. Sometimes, I felt the bookish language was insufficient to succeed in real life. But anyway, I persevered and kept working on my goal, and today, I have finally achieved a position I always wanted to reach. I dominated my subject knowledge. Today, my hard work, strengths, and patience have paid me a high income, and I have a high status and respect in society. So always be ready for the competition. Your competitors are standing before you, and you must prove to them that you are bigger than everything. "

That day, I felt so motivated listening to Mr. Akash's talk, but a few facts ignorantly hit my mind, I didn't notice those hard facts at that time

But later, I did; what were those facts from his motivating talk? Facts were;

a) Life is difficult.
b) Life is struggling and torturing initially; after that, no problem.
c) Bookish language doesn't work in real life.
d) Finally, we reach, and the journey ends.
e) He earned a lot of money and status.
f) He said he dominated the subject knowledge
g) Credits were given for hard work, strength and patience.
h) No-one else contributed
i) He did everything alone
j) Competition is waiting for us
k) Competitors are waiting for us
l) We have to prove ourselves
m) We have to be bigger than our competitors

There was nothing wrong with Mr. Akash's talk; it sounded motivating. However, there is a difference between motivation and inspiration.

Motivation is more factual and logical, whereas Inspiration is like kinesthetic: it can be felt, rejoiced, and enjoyed. Motivation and Inspiration are both important, but when given only one, something is lost in the game.

For instance, let's take an imaginary character named "Mr. Akash V2" (Version 2) and put them into my same college story;

...someone from my class asked him,
"How has been your journey to success, Mr. Akash V2?'

Akash V2 stated, "It has been an amazing experience for me. The initial 5 years were more challenging, but all the important success lessons were learned there only. Thank God to my teachers who showered their knowledge and taught me real-life skills to face the real world. The way my family and loved ones supported me, I realized I was more powerful than before. The whole journey has been a dream come true for me. I am still on the journey; I know I must serve more of society and the loved ones who have always been there for me. I can say today that my hard work, strengths and patience paid me money, but all these values were engraved by my masters, gurus and the god I always trusted. Finally, I want to say that success is easy when you love your work, yourself and the people around you. In this journey, you don't need to prove yourself, improve yourself".

Did you experience what is – flirting with the right brain – approach?

Imagine if Mr. Akash had spoken the same content that day. What could have happened? I know these are the imaginary lines of Mr. Akash V2, but there is nothing wrong with going back and imagining the version 2 talk in Mr. Akash's voice. Because this version 2 sounds equally motivating and impeccably inspiring, too. Listeners can feel more this version 2. Let me explain Version 2-point wise explanation, but this time, feel the tinge of flirting in the idea generation;

a)   Life is amazing.
b)   Life is challenging but insightful for a life-long learner.
c)   Life-long learners become more powerful day by day
d)   Teachers' contribution is non-negotiable
e)   Life skills will support you, apart from subject knowledge
f)   He is living a dream life, and still, he is in the journey only
g)   He was counting his loved one's contributions
h)   He was down to earth throughout his talk
i)   He wants to serve more and add more value to people's lives.

j) He credited his masters, gurus and God, as they engraved the value system inside.
k) He said success is easy when you love your work
l) He said, "Love others, even competitors."
m) Finally, he concluded, focus on improving, not proving anyone.

So, when you speak, have you ever checked your version? Is it only Version 1, which is practical, mature, and organized, or do you follow Version 2, which is equally practical, mature, and organized but also imaginative, heart-touching, and easily progressive? Wow, it sounds so nice: "easily progressive." These two words make the journey to progress sound easier and more beautiful.

Now, the time has come to choose Version 2. This is not an A.I. focused (Artificial Intelligence), but R.I. focused (Real Intelligence). A.I. is powerful, but R.I. is powerful + Likable.

Power comes from logic and facts. In short, our left brain can make our lives easy with powerful inventions. At the same time, likability comes from emotion, trust, and peace, which come from the right brain. We need to sharpen both our brains, Left and right.

Imagine many readers are reading this book. There is no doubt that some are logical, and some are imaginative. As a writer, thinker, and author, I need to use my Version 2 mindset here, i.e., use my logic and magic. Here, magic talks about feelings, emotions, sentiments, etc. If I use both my brains for my idea generation, I could touch the minds of logical readers and the hearts of emotional readers, too.

This approach would produce Versatile Communication Skills. Version 2 is more versatile than Version 1. Versatility is important for creating excitement and curiosity. It also helps create and sustain something that is not new right now.

This book resonates with version 2 of our personality and communication skills, but it is more extensive than we have discussed. So, I recommend that all readers read different information sources and get maximum details on the Left and Right Brains. Flirting with others requires different skills, but flirting with yourself always requires special skills. Everyone needs to sharpen their right-brain thinking habits because this is not popular.

Speakers who use the right brain are bold enough, proactive and happy. These speakers are unique and convincing. These Right brain-activated speakers experiment with their vocabulary, emotions and voice modulations. Right Brain speakers never use negative words like, "I can't do it", "This is impossible", This can't be done by anyone", "Why me god?", "This is not my cup of tea", "I don't get what I want" "My life has no charm!" etc.

Here, right-brain-activated speakers mean speakers who use logic with their left brain and magic with their right brain. These speakers are versatile, powerful, and exciting. Their personalities are so impressive that income follows them even when they are not doing anything (passive income).

Now, the right brain answers to the activity – Making a square with four equal parts:

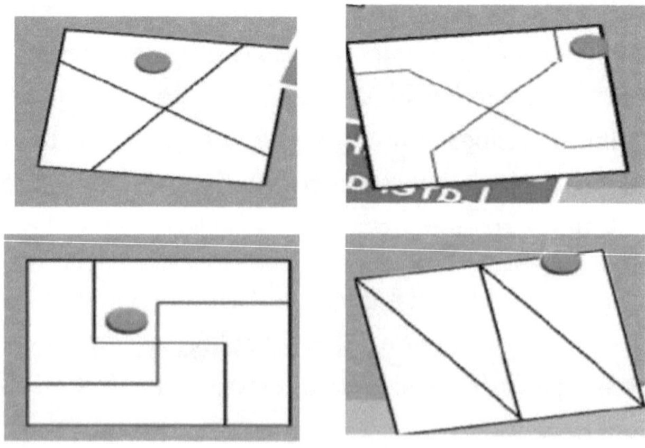

Truth - 11
ENSURE YOU SPEAK LIKE
A HOST, NOT A GHOST

Can a ghost be an impressive communicator? definitely not!

Does anyone want to speak like a ghost? No way!

Who are ghosts, by the way? Are they real?

Yes! They are real!

I am not talking about "ghosts who are dead" but about real-life ghosts.

We would never want to be a GHOST in real life and hurt others, right?
But still, we never know; sometimes, we behave in ways that hurt people.
Why are we not aligned with our own values?

How do we know if we are ghosts or hosts?

Who are GHOSTS?

G – Giving

H – Honest

O – Opinion

S – Straightforwardly

T – Then & There

Do you give straightforwardly honest opinions to everyone?

Are you being straightforward every time?

I remember the year was around 2002. I was in Jamshedpur, the steel city. I was born and brought up in Jamshedpur only, with little information for those who don't know me personally. There is a renowned park called "Jubilee Park", one of the most beautiful parks in India. So, one fine sunny morning, one of my cousin's brothers, Pushpak, and I went there to enjoy. Pushpak is from one of the metro cities in India, and he heard about Jubilee Park many times from me, so he wanted to see it. He always boasts himself as an honest reviewer. According to him, he speaks with honesty and always gives honest feedback. So that day when we both visited the park, I was super excited, as that park was the best park in the city. I asked him, "Brother, how did I like it? Isn't it big and beautiful?". He replied, "Don't ask me; you might not like my feedback. You know I am honest and straightforward while giving feedback".

I was gobsmacked and wanted to listen to him. I asked, "Didn't you like it? Please give me genuine feedback," and then he started,

"Honestly, it didn't meet my expectations. You were so hyperbole about this park. So, I thought it would be more beautiful, but I am disappointed. There are better parks in my city".

I replied, "Ok, bro, thanks for your honest review".

I received his feedback openly, although it was not directly directed at me. Still, I felt hurt. I have my own likings for my city and the places where I spent my childhood. It is so personal to me, and someone, in the name of honesty and straightforwardness, directly attacked my emotions. I didn't like it. I know my brother didn't mean it or didn't want to hurt me, but he hurt me.

Many times, we like people, but we don't like their thoughts or values, right?

So, should we keep in touch with them? Why not? We are all different, and this makes us unique. However, being with so-called realistic people and getting their realistic feedback is not easy. One so-called honest question to all honest and straightforward people is, "Are you open to straightforward comments being given to you?"

You might say now you will take it openly, but there is a difference between honesty on the spot and honesty spot-on.

What is honesty and straightforwardness?

Honesty means "not lying to people," my brother also did that. He didn't lie; he just spoke honestly on the spot like a GHOST" (giving honest opinion straightforwardly then and there). What do you all think about this "honest Ghost"?

Logically, my brother expressed his feelings and gave honest feedback, but emotionally, could he respond even better than a ghost? I guess the answer is "yes."

He could have chosen the HOST- approach rather than a GHOST approach.

Now, who are HOSTS?

H – Honest

O – Opinion

S – Strategically &

T – Timely (at right time)

HOSTS are people who give honest feedback and know "how to give honest feedback honestly—the right way and also at the right time."

Sometimes, we give positive feedback on the spot, and sometimes, later, it may not be immediately if we give negative feedback, but constructively. This does two things: First, it helps the person feel good, and after some time, the same person understands what needs to be done next to improve. Here, honesty won, but not the on-the-spot honesty, but honesty spot-on (honesty with some strategy).

This is an ideal example of "Honesty Spot-On."

Imagine the same story about the city of Jamshedpur, my cousin, and me. But this time, let's modify my cousin Pushpak's response (not real, but modified).

Pushpak's strategic, honest reply could have been: "Wow, brother, this is big and beautiful. I even learned that our first Prime Minister, the late Pd. JL Nehru inaugurated this park, am I right? Jamshedpur is a small city, but it has amazing places, roads, and other amenities. Even the people are nice and well-behaved. When you used to talk about this park, I was so eager to come, and today, finally, I am so fortunate to be here."

No exaggeration or No hyperbole. Simple answer honesty spot-on.

But what's the background psychology behind the Strategic Response of the modified Pushpak'k response? (not real but modified)

Background psychology: Even Pushpak's city has more amazing parks, but those parks don't belong to this story. They have their own stories. Every park has its own small or big stories. Let's learn to see the positives in people, places and things around us. Speak negatives if it is important to be spoken, but ensure your words on "those negative points" are honest and at the right time, and multiple positive points should precede it as a protected shield to the listener.

Many students speak during the Public Speaking session. I often see candidates speaking impeccably, with praiseworthy vocabulary and impressive body language. I stand for them and give them a standing ovation. But many times, even though I know the performance didn't deserve one, I still stand and give a standing ovation.

But why? Because we don't only stand and clap when we see "Top Performances", sometimes "Top Improvements" should also be appreciated.

Understand my intentions. I often stand to make participants feel "how beautifully and dedicatedly they have been working on their communication and improving in the last few days." Their performance may not be perfect, but their improvement has been incredibly positive.

Here, improvement level means "the percentage of recent enhancement being seen during the speaking performance," so I stand. I do not show off my honesty and make participants feel inferior; I start with positive feedback and points evaluated during the presentation to make the participants feel comfortable and aspiring. After sharing all the positive feedback, I start sharing with the action areas to be worked upon.

For instance, Condition: The Speaker's performance was not up to the mark, but it was better than the last.

GHOST'S HONEST FEEDBACK ON THE SPOT:

Ghost to participant: This is very disappointing! I didn't like it. Last time, I also told you to work on your facial expressions, smile, eye contact, and hand gestures. I haven't seen any positive changes in the last 14 days.

This feedback will surely make the speaker feel disappointed and hopeless.

After-effect: The receiver of the message will not feel inspired. Hence, future rectifications will be at risk.

HOST'S HONEST FEEDBACK SPOTS ON:

Host to participant: Wow, this is amazing! What a comeback! Your body language was absent last time, but great improvements have been seen today. This is called regular transformation.

This feedback will make him feel comfortable and relieved.

However, after I finish with the inspiring positive messages, I will also share their genuine action areas to be worked on so I can continue discussing what was unsatisfactory.

After-effect: The receiver of the message will feel inspired, and the focus will be on the next course of action, i.e. body language and Neuroscience.

GHOST's honesty is more upfront, and HOST's honesty is more accepting, inspiring and heroic.

GHOSTS show off their honesty, but HOSTS show care with their honesty.

GHOSTS do three things right, but 4th thing goes for a toss;

First, GHOSTS love to learn values.

Second, they act on those values and

Third, they respect values in self and others too.

But the fourth thing they can't manage well and that is –

"They demean people who don't do the same, and as a result, GHOSTS become arrogant". Imagine, even after being honest, that GHOSTS fail honesty. Because sometimes "honesty needs to be a little strategic".

HOSTS do five things right:

First, HOSTS love to learn values.

Second, they act on those values

Third, they respect values in self and others too.

Fourth, they know the timing well. They know that the right things are like bullets that can hurt people, so if the timing is right, the bullet can be replaced with flower petals. HOSTS know very well that my rights may not be other people's. My right time may not be the same as another person's. So, respecting and considering other people's viewpoints can transform GHOSTS into HOSTS.

And finally, fifth,

HOSTS self-correct rather than correct others. Whenever anything goes wrong, they ask the first person to ask a question, i.e., "to self." They are open to training and sometimes retraining.

Yes! HOSTS know well that "what they know may be right today, but not tomorrow. So, they are always flexible and accept present-day, positive, or progressive trends."

So, are you considering yourself as a HOST-Communicator?

If yes, you must enjoy healthy relationships with others. You are caring, positive, and inspiring. You could be an amazing Life Coach or a counsellor for somebody who needs it. You manage values, people, and timing well.

You don't show off but focus on doing things right. When anyone boasts about you in front of others, you stop them or segue to another topic. You prefer to work, talk and act right in silence.

Do you belong to the Team of HOSTS? If not, or maybe partially, you do, what's stopping you?

Don't you want to be surrounded by positive proximity? Don't you want to create an eco-system with all Value centric people? Don't you want a healthy relationship with everyone with a lifetime connection? Don't you want people to set your example in relationship management? Don't you want others to notice you when you talk or be silent? Don't you want people to come to you and learn relationship and feedback techniques?

Yes or no? Your answer will determine your personality, communication skills, and heroic life.

A heroic personality is not just one of beauty, boldness, and prosperity; it impresses people with your character, values and communication style.

Impression is important because Impression is a "New Income"

Like dears and antelopes, known for their horns, humans are known for their way of speaking. Speaking decides the impression we make while talking to others, and finally …

The impression we make creates "our income," and our income often decides relationships, lifestyle, and progress in life.

So, every story we listen to or experience starts with one thing: Communication Skills. Communication skills were never optional but an integral and essential part of human life.

All the very best!

PHASE 3: CONCLUSION

The final words from the author

Final - 01
A WORM'S EYE VIEW

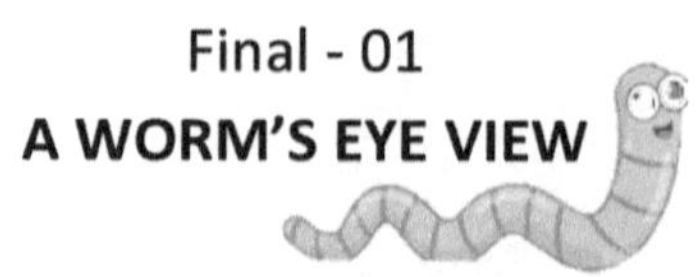

Let me explain **15 Impressive Deep Value Systems** one can live with;

1. Speak what is right! If saying "No" is right, say No with positive body language.

2. Speak with self-respect. Don't talk negatively about yourself, not even in your thoughts.

3. Speak being grounded. Your talk should inspire, not conspire.

4. To impress, be happy first. Happy faces are always noticed.

5. To impress, use the right brain. Speak with a positive attitude towards life.

6. We communicate effectively; this is not automatic but deliberate.

7. RAS activates Luck, and lucky people are more impressive communicators.

8. Progressive people speak less, but when they do, they ensure others progress.

9. Speak only when silence is a sin and your integrity provokes you to speak.

10. If anger and jealousy are inside, they surely will come outside while speaking.

11. If love, peace and happiness are inside, they surely will come outside while speaking.

12. Be soft like a kid and powerful like a person with Integrity, an amazing and impressive combination.

13. Power personality is always impressive. TQPS is the secret behind real power.

14. Bosses who have integrity & dignity always like employees with the same values.

15. Bosses who lack integrity & dignity are scared of employees who have these two qualities.

Final - 02
A BIRD'S EYE VIEW

Let me explain **15 Impressive Aerial Findings that** one can excel with;

1. To impress, ensure your talk complements others' dignity.

2. To impress, keep your smile intact throughout your talk.

3. Even if you are an introvert, speak with others. No one would judge you.

4. Even if you are an extrovert, go beyond your nature – speak what is needed and start listening to people more.

5. Be an ambivert and balance your speaking and listening quotient.

6. Whether in your office or at home, practise being a nice speaker and respecting others.

7. Learn five new words every week and practise speaking with those five words.

8. Practise Public speaking at least once a week.

9. While speaking, lean forward towards the speaker to show interest.

10. While listening, do nodding. Speakers will love you, even trust you.

11. Use both hands while speaking. Your gestures show power, impact and celebration.

12. While shaking hands, look at the person, smile and lean forward.

13. While shaking hands, feel the touch and hold the hand firmly.

14. While talking, listening or shaking hands, eye contact should be intact.

15. Wear presentable and value dressing because look matters when you speak. Anything that matters in our communication can't be ignored but learnt. So, practice communication even if you are a master at it.

Final - 03
ACKNOWLEDGEMENTS

Let me express my deepest thanks to all my gurus, masters, family members, book readers, and every member of my IDQ Value Adder family (coaches and students), who made me what I am today. Without their input and presence, I couldn't imagine myself, my position, or my achievements. I owe you everything that I have achieved to date.

Special Thanks to my Gurus: Sri Krishna (Bhagwat Geeta), Sri Ramakrishna, Swami Vivekananda, Shive Khera, Sat & Siri, Robin Sharma, Rajiv Talreja, Sandeep Maheswari, Praveen Verma, Sanjay Ranjan, Sister Shivani, Jim Rohn, Steve Jobs, Tony Robbins, Sam Cawthorn, Edward De Bono, Mahatma Gandhi, Stephen R Covey, Dr Wayne Dyer, Bob Proctor, Robert Greene, Dale Carnegie, Napoleon Hill, Louise Hay, Robert Kiyosaki, Nicholas Boothman, Rhonda Byrne, Joseph Murphy, Michael Losier, Carolyn Boyes, George S Clason, Zig Ziglar, Nick Vujicic, Dr. Richard Bandler (NLP) and everyone who has directly indirectly impacted my life.

Thanks to my family members for their contributions: Kartik K Mandal (father), Shila Mandal (mother), Pratichi M Shukla (wife), Shravya (daughter), Pramit (son), Ganesh Mandal (uncle), Tumpa Das (sister), Raja Mandal (brother), and everyone who has always been there for me.

Thanks for the image courtesy:

Canva.com, stockphoto.com, shutterstock.com, freepik.com, dreamstime.com, alamy.com, flickr.com, istockphoto.com, IDQ Value Adder's Image gallery.

Thanks to all my pre-launch readers:

H. Bharathi Bai Pawar, Namita Adhikary Patra, Deepali Atmaram Kolhe, Bhavana Dewangan, Sujata Waghmare, Naturally Neha, Subarna Mittra, Tamasi Mandal, Papiya Karji,Farha Naveed, Bandita Pradhan, Tarasis Adak, Shelly kalia, Soma Paul, M V Naresh Kumar, Ramu, Preeti Srivastava, Iti Dey, Sweta Singh,Shalini Tripathi,Nibedita Bhattacharyya,Haleema Pervez, Nanditha Suman, Suma Santagoudar, Rinkan Hazra, Ishteyaque Ahmad, Preeti Sagar,Aquleema Azmat,Bharti Gursahaney, Indrani Chatterjee, Manpreet Kaur Wahi, Sundaresan, Sanat Kumar Mishra,Sonia Bishnu, Ujwala Gore, Laxman Thorat, Mahesh Kandukoori, Roni Kumar, Lalit Kumar, Hem Narayan Das, Shyam kanhaiya Vishwakarma, Sushil Kumar, Manju Raheja, Sukhadeo Vinayak Ghegade, Sudesna Das, Shalini Shukla, Sanchita Vinsulkar,Ragini Ray,Dipankar Haldar,Janavi, Mahesh Bamaney, Raghwendra Kumar Choudhary, Mahesh Kandukoori, Pankaj Sharma, L Shanthi, Murugesh B K, Abhilash Sawla, Vandana Jalmi, Aruna Pawar, Simran Khatwani, Sweta Dutta Mondal, Seema Rao, Smita Santosh Kadam, Suman Shriwas, Hira Lal, Lekha Khodiyar, Tanoj Rai, Nibha,Mohd.jahangeer, Pratyay Acharya, Jagannath Panda,Lakshmi Rupa R,Sanjay Sengar,Nikhil Thiruvantheri, Mamta Tyagi,Soma Ghosh,Rajasri Srikanth, Renu Bisht, Banabindu Chakma, R Amudha, Ravi Kumar Singh, Mushini Venkata Naresh Kumar, Phani Madhavi,Parveen Malhotra, Sumayya Jabeen,Raju Chatterjee, Thirunam Padma, Pankaj singh Chauhan, Shivani, Komal Singh, Khateeb Kulsum, Dr Rahoul Ranawwat, Bhavani, Dipti Singh, Vrushali Tiwaskar, Subir Mandal,Dr.Babita Choudhury, Bandana Pattanaik, Kakali Bose Sen, Shivamurthy Kariyappa,Yugandhar Rajamahanti, Rashmi H E, Shradha Pathak, Anupam Prarthy, Runa,Sundari, Shashikant Patel, Anjana Pegu, Thamizh selvi, Jyoti Naik, Aniket Anant Patil, Kavya Shewale, Dupinderjit kaur, Allabakksh Mujawor, Shyam Kanhaiya Vishwakarma, Navin Upadhyay, Sneha Chandrapal, Lata Pable, Bhabeshwari Kalita,T Padma, Dr. Itishree Prusty, Shibili K,Rajasri Srikant, Bharati Gursahaney,Rahul Ranawwat, Sanghamitra Dasgupta,Manish Waghmare, Rekha Tyagi, Anu, Seema Kumari, Kaavya Shewale, Ranjit Thakuria, Hem Raj, Mitra Nandi, Mehrin Chopda, Anu Thakur, Smita Hatekar, Rajiv Bharti, Arun Gupta, Dipannita Chakraborty, Aswini Kumar Das, Bimal Kumar, Dr. Chhaya Mishra, Rufi Mohasin Malvl

www.ingramcontent.com/pod-product-compliance
Lightning Source LLC
Chambersburg PA
CBHW062150150726
47991CB00006B/2225

9798896990871